Thanks to Lt. Col. Eric M. Solander, S Sgt. Michael S. Harland,
and the people of the United States Air Force.
Compiled and edited by Ross A. Howell, Jr.
Designed by Marilyn F. Appleby and John F. Grant.
Photographs copyright © 1984 by Mark Meyer. All rights reserved.
Introduction copyright © 1984 by Charles E. Yeager. All rights reserved.
Illustrations courtesy of Pilot Press.
This book, or any portions thereof, may not be reproduced in any form
without permission of the publisher, Thomasson-Grant, Inc.
Photography may not be reproduced without permission of Mark Meyer.
Library of Congress Catalog Number 83-51813 ISBN 0-934738-62-9
Printed and bound in Japan by Dai Nippon Printing Co., Ltd.
Any inquiries should be directed to Thomasson-Grant, Inc.,
One Morton Drive, Suite 500, Charlottesville, Virginia, 22901,
telephone (804) 977-1780.
Softbound edition copyright © 1989 by Thomasson-Grant, Inc.

Thomasson-Grant

WINGS

Photography by Mark Meyer

Introduction by Chuck Yeager

MY EXPERIENCE with United States Air Force aircraft covers nearly 40 years. I've been fortunate to participate in the evolution of many of our modern jet aviation systems — and I've had a good deal to do with how those systems turned out.

I began flying school in 1942 with Ryan PT-22s, little low-wing monoplanes. In those days the method of training pilots was to mask off the airspeed indicator below 80 miles per hour. You could see when the airspeed needle got above 80 mph so you wouldn't overstress the airplane, but masking that airspeed indicator was very beneficial. It made you learn to fly the airplane, land it, and do your pattern work strictly by feel and sound.

After getting my wings, I went into P-39s for about 400 hours. There I began to develop the skills of a fighter pilot—dogfighting, skip-bombing, dive-bombing, air-to-ground gunnery, and air-to-air gunnery. You had to learn how to "lead" a target because we flew with the old ring-and-bead gunsight. That gunsight was in the T-6 trainers, where we learned our first gunnery, and in the P-47 and P-38 fighters. In leading a target, you had to do everything by instinct.

Then I went into P-51s. Most of our aircraft in World War II — fighters, bombers, trainers — were reciprocating-engine powered, that is, they used internal-combustion, piston engines. Most bombers, cargo aircraft, and training airplanes used radial engines — the cylinders radiated from a central drive axle. Fighters used both radial and in-line engines. The P-47 "Thunderbolt," for example, used a big radial engine, while the P-51 "Mustang" used an in-line engine. The in-line engines were liquid-cooled, requiring a radiator. That radiator made your airplane vulnerable. One small bullet through it, and you lost all your coolant and your airplane. The P-47 was better than the P-51 for air-to-ground support because its radial engine was air-cooled. You could have cylinders shot off that big old radial engine, and it would still fly home.

By the summer of 1944, the first lead-computing gunsight was developed. Called the K-14 gunsight, it was installed in P-51s and P-47s—the two major airplanes we flew in the European theater late in WWII. The pilot set the wingspan of the airplane he was fighting on a manual spanner selector—you would know in your head that a German Me-109 was 30 to 31 feet; a Ju-188, maybe 70 or 80 feet. Through a system of gyros and rheostats in the throttle, you put the bead on the middle of the enemy airplane and adjusted the spanner diamonds to put them on its wing tips. The gunsight would compute the lead and aim your airplane the proper distance in front of your target. The K-14 made it much easier to shoot an airplane down during maneuvering flight and at 90 degrees deflection.

The P-51 was probably the best prop fighter in WWII. Although it was very effective, it was about the last Air Force prop fighter. German development of the Me-262, which came into combat in 1944, signaled the beginning of the era of jet aviation. The Me-262 was very successful. It could reach about .8 Mach number, or 80 percent of the speed of sound, and had about an hour's range.

Here we began to see what speed meant in the realm of aerial warfare. The Me-262 could fly up to high altitude, where it was very effective against our B-17 and B-24 bombers. It was also effective in dogfighting, as long as it didn't try to turn as tightly as the prop-fighters. Fortunately, German commanders decided to use the Me-262s in air-to-ground warfare. They were not dedicated to air defense — shooting down bombers. Had they been, WWII probably would have lasted another year, until we could get the P-80, our first USAF combat jet, into the theater.

With jet aviation came the problems of the "sound barrier." A P-51 prop-fighter diving from high altitude with the throttle wide open could reach a speed of about .8 Mach number. That was as fast as you could go in a P-51, a P-47, or any other prop airplane, because they had such thick wings. At .8 Mach number, we began to get shock waves on the airplane—we began to run into buffeting and loss of control. At this point, 1944, the Air Force initiated a research aircraft program called XS-1. "X" designated research, "S," supersonic, and "1" indicated that it was the first contract let for a supersonic research airplane.

With the X-1 program in 1947, we found that airplanes — if they have a fixed horizontal stabilizer with elevators — lose elevator effectiveness as they approach the speed of sound. We lost elevator effectiveness in the X-1, but were able to maintain control of the airplane through the speed of sound by means of its horizontal stabilizer, which had the capability of changing angle of incidence. Consequently, we learned that if you wanted to operate at the speed of sound, your airplane had to have a "flying tail," that is, the entire horizontal stabilizer must be maneuverable when you pull back on the control stick.

With that knowledge we built the F-86, which had a flying tail. It was pitted against the Russian MiG-15 in the Korean War. We shot down roughly ten MiG-15s for every F-86 we lost. Later, while I was flight-testing a MiG-15 we had gotten when a North Korean pilot defected, we found out that the Russians hadn't learned what we had in aerodynamic research. The MiG-15 had a fixed horizontal stabilizer with elevators and could not maneuver above .93 Mach number.

A fighter airplane, obviously, must have a great deal of maneuverability to do its job. In the F-100, we discovered that when an airplane begins to fly at supersonic speed, you get "supersonic flow" over the whole aircraft. That tremendous flow of air almost locks the airplane into place—it becomes so stable that it's not very maneuverable. We backed off and said, "OK, in order for our aircraft to be maneuverable at supersonic speeds, they've got to have flight control surfaces that make them less stable at subsonic speeds." This led to a problem that stayed with us through a few generations of fighters. The airplane in the subsonic speed range was so unstable that you had trouble flying it precisely. That brought about the installation of "stability augmentation" systems—pitch, yaw, and roll dampeners on our control systems.

It was a new technique of flying. When the airplane was at subsonic speeds, dampeners made it fly acceptably. As you went to supersonic speeds, air-data computers decreased the effectiveness of the dampeners, making the airplane more maneuverable. This is the way we built the F-100, the F-104, the F-101, right on through to airplanes in the F-4 speed range. We had to make the F-4 so unstable at subsonic speeds in order to have it maneuverable at Mach 2, that even with stability augmentation, the airplane—if you exceeded the parameters of pitch or yaw—would snap, and it was difficult to recover from the resultant "departure," or spin. That was one of the worst areas we got ourselves into.

This brought about, by the early '70s, the "fly-by-wire" control systems. Our technology had reached the point where we could install an on-board computer that, by means of servomechanisms, could fly an airplane. Through his controls, the pilot says to the computer, "Give me a so-many G turn," or "Give me this rate of roll or yaw," and the computer analyzes its flight data and moves the control surfaces to give the pilot what he asks for—within carefully determined limits.

We program the on-board computer and say, "All right, we've built a very unstable aircraft here. It is going to be very maneuverable both at subsonic speeds and at supersonic speeds. But we never want this airplane to exceed a certain angle of attack; we don't want it to exceed a certain yaw angle, or a certain roll rate, or a combination thereof." That results in a system of checks and balances, so that regardless of what the pilot asks for, the computer is never going to let him get outside the aircraft's acceptable stability envelope. Consequently, we can build a very unstable airplane, moving the center of gravity back—giving us tremendous pitch rates and maneuvering capabilities.

The F-16 was the first production fly-by-wire airplane. In the early F-16s, we had a "fixed force" sidearm control. You didn't move the stick; pressure from your hand produced electrical impulses that entered the computer through a "strain gauge." It was a problem for new pilots, because humans aren't calibrated in force. Since they couldn't tell how many pounds of pressure they were applying, they couldn't assess their control positions. Of course, with fly-by-wire the computer is only going to give the pilot the control position that's appropriate for the maneuver he selects, but we decided to go to a movable force stick—the sidearm control moves about an inch back and an inch forward. When the pilot hits the stop, he knows that he is probably at full-up control.

Going to the fly-by-wire system in the F-16 uncovered new problems. First, with an analog computer in the flight control system and a digital computer in the weapons management system, we had some incompatibility. Second, the fly-by-wire system requires a very stable electrical source to give precise inputs to the computer. Everything had to be very finely calibrated—if you lost a generator, or if you had false pulses in your electrical systems, then you had problems. The F-16 has no back-up system for the computer flight controls. In the development phase, we lost a few aircraft. The F-18 and F-20 use digital computers for the flight control systems that are compatible with the digital computers in the weapons management systems, and they employ a center control stick instead of the sidearm controller, making back-up flight control systems possible. If you lose your computer or the power source to your computer, you can go to an electrical or a hydraulic back-up flight control system.

With an on-board computer, you have a large amount of stored information available to the pilot. We were able to progress from the lead-computing gunsights that required manual adjustment to computerized electrical or radar-data systems that feed information to lead-computing gunsights automatically. We also developed the "Head-Up Display" (HUD), which projects all flight data the pilot needs up to the windshield—angle of attack, airspeed, altitude, even what weapons are on the airplane. The pilot doesn't have to look down inside the cockpit at all.

We've been able to improve our modern inertial navigation systems (INS) with ring-laser gyros. Weapons systems and navigation systems depend on computer data from the INS to get proper accuracy in navigation and weapons delivery. If you're sitting with a "cold" airplane and the notice comes to "scramble," you've got to put power on your INS with the old gyros, get them lined up and the memory loaded—let it find out where it is. That takes a minimum of four minutes. All that time you're sitting there on the runway. The new ring-laser INS with no gyros takes only 22 seconds to full alignment. You can go out to your aircraft, turn the power on, start the INS, start your engine, and by the time the engine's running, you're ready to go with a full bank of reference data.

Most airplanes from WWII through the F-4 were designed to pull 7.33 Gs. You could pull more, but the airplane would begin to bend. With control systems for maneuvering at supersonic speeds and the development of very powerful engines giving thrust-to-weight ratios approaching one, we could design aircraft with the capability of sustaining nine Gs of constant maneuvering at low altitude.

Development of a nine-G aircraft like the F-16 emphasized a problem we ran into back in WWII—pilots blacking out because of G forces. The WWII prop fighters could pull over four Gs in banking from a 350 to 400 mph dive. Everything inside you feels four times its normal weight. The vessels in your legs and lower extremities expand from the weight of your blood. As the vessels expand, blood begins to drain into your lower body, overcoming your heart's ability to pump blood to your brain. First, a pilot loses his peripheral vision. If he's pulling more than four Gs, as time elapses, he loses his vision. If he holds back on the control stick for ten or 15 seconds—continues to pull those Gs—then he becomes unconscious.

In WWII, my squadron of P-51s was equipped with "anti-G suits." The first one was an air suit that you wore below the waist. It had a bladder against your stomach and bladders against the thighs and calves of your legs. As you pulled about two Gs in maneuvering the airplane, compressed air blew those bladders up tightly, kept your blood vessels from expanding, and held the blood up toward your heart. If you normally blacked out pulling four Gs, with the anti-G suit, you could withstand about six Gs. Those suits enabled us to follow a German Me-109 who might be pulling a five-G maneuver. He would be blacked out, but still flying the airplane by feel. You could keep your awareness through that same turn, track him, and shoot him down. The Germans never developed production G-suits during WWII. The ones we wore in the P-51s are basically the same G-suits that we wear today in F-15s and F-16s.

Propulsion systems are tremendously important in modern aviation. The P-59, the first American jet, flew in 1942; the P-80 followed in 1944. Engines in those early jets were quite simple. We got into more advanced jet engines when the F-86 came out—we went to axial-flow compressor jet engines instead of centrifugal-flow compressor jet engines. In the late '40s and early '50s, we started developing engines with afterburners, which increased thrust dramatically. Afterburners used a great deal of fuel, but they enabled the F-100 to be the first airplane to fly straight and level at supersonic speeds.

As airplanes approached the Mach 2 speed range, jet engine design became more complex to increase fuel efficiency. Until the development of the F-104, our jet engines were "constant-geometry" engines—compressor parts and intake ducts were fixed. In the F-104 we went to "variable-inlet guide vanes" that could be adjusted to change the amount of air deflected into the compressor blades. We had learned that when you're operating out beyond Mach 2, you start getting shock waves in the intake ducts. If that shock wave moves back in the engine, it causes a compressor stall. Variable-inlet geometry—like in the F-4 and the F-15—keeps the shock wave from entering the engine.

These complex propulsion systems had many

parts and were hard to maintain. The Pratt and Whitney PF-100 engine in the F-15 and F-16 probably "bleeds" more energy out of an ounce of fuel than any other engine. But since it is so complex and finely balanced, any damage or erosion to a compressor blade can cause an imbalance. If there is a disturbance in the air coming through the intake, you can get stagnation stalls or compressor stalls. For the F-15, the engine problems were not so serious because you had two engines. In the F-16, they were very serious, because you had a single engine.

We had spent years in research and development building fighters that were capable of more and more speed. But we realized that you don't need all that speed. Most dogfighting is done from .9 to 1.2 Mach. Anytime you operate out beyond 2.2 Mach number, about all you're doing is using fuel. If a guy's running from you, you can launch a missile that will normally go out about two Machs faster than your airspeed and catch whatever is running from you. In the old P-51s, we used to dogfight, turn and turn, and try to get on another guy's tail. But with the development of new air-to-air missile systems, you don't need tail-end position. The guy who wins a dogfight today is the guy who rotates, aims, and shoots first.

Rather than continue to build complex, variable-geometry systems capable of higher and higher speeds, we decided to build simpler, more reliable fixed-geometry intake systems, like the F-16 and F-18. Fixed-geometry intake systems limit airplanes to Mach 2 speeds. But they enable us to use propulsion systems today that are like those of the 1940s—very simple engines, fewer parts, easy to maintain, very strong. A new engine like the General Electric 404 may not bleed as much energy out of an ounce of fuel as a PF-100, but it's not susceptible to compressor stalls or compressor stagnation. In the F-15 or F-16, a pilot has to pay close attention to what he's doing with the throttle if he's maneuvering the airplane. With the new engines, you never have to worry about it—you can be flying backwards at idle and get instantaneous response.

Of course, titanium and other alloys in the 1960s made it possible for us to continue to explore the realm of speed. An airplane flying at Mach 2 experiences skin temperatures of about 100 degrees centigrade. As an airplane goes to Mach 3 speed, its skin temperature gets up to 600 or 700 degrees. With titanium and stainless steel, we were able to build aircraft structures that could survive those heat extremes and operate out at Mach 3. Two airplanes developed in the '60s had that capability—the B-70 and the SR-71. Designed to be operated as a bomber, the B-70 was cancelled. It was too difficult and costly to design an accurate weapons delivery system from the altitude —above 70,000 feet—that Mach 3 speed requires.

The SR-71 evolved from the YF-12, a fighter-interceptor designed to carry long-range air-to-air missiles. Like the B-70, the YF-12 was discontinued. But when Gary Powers' U-2 was shot down by a surface-to-air missile over Russia, our need for a high-speed strategic reconnaissance aircraft became apparent. With the YF-12 airframe, we were able to develop the SR-71, putting us in a speed range beyond the capabilities of most air-to-air and ground-to-air missiles. Recently the utility of the SR-71 has decreased. Space observation is an accepted method of reconnoitering over another country, and more advanced missile systems have brought the SR-71 into the vulnerable arena. But data on systems, structures, and partial-bypass propulsion came out of both the B-70 and SR-71 programs that greatly increased our knowledge in operating at Mach 3 and beyond.

As a test pilot at Edwards Air Force Base, I participated in the development of in-flight refueling in the '50s. With jet aircraft across our inventory —fighter, bomber, cargo, and reconnaissance— we had airplanes that consumed a great deal of fuel and were relatively limited in range. Since USAF aircraft in all the major commands must be able to operate all over the world, we realized that we had to refine the technique of in-flight refueling.

In-flight refueling was not a new concept. Many people remember the flight of the "Question Mark" in the '20s that used "in-flight refueling" crossing the United States—another airplane flew up and let a hose down or dropped a can of gasoline on a rope to the "receiver" airplane. When I was flying in-flight refueling missions in fighters and training Strategic Air Command boom operators in the first B-47 bomber at March Field, we employed a similar technique—the "probe-and-drogue." In that system the mother aircraft, the tanker, reeled out a hose with a cone or funnel on it, and the receiver aircraft had a probe. The receiver flew up and shoved the probe into the drogue receptacle. Then the mother ship would turn on the fuel pump and transfer fuel.

The fuel transfer rate with that system was relatively slow—it was sufficient for fighters, but not for bombers. Also, since bombers couldn't fly as precise a formation as fighters, it was difficult to insert the probe. That led us to develop the "flying-boom" refueling system.

In boom refueling, the receiver aircraft flies up in formation. On the rear of the tanker is a boom with maneuverable vanes. A boom operator inside the mother ship flies the boom down and inserts it in the receptacle of the receiver. With this method we are able to transfer fuel at five or six times the rate that we could with the drogue system. Since many of our fighters were already equipped for drogue refueling, we stuck those systems onto the boom and used it in refueling fighters. We employed the boom system for bombers.

Finally, with the F-4 fighters, we realized that it would be simpler to employ the boom system in all our aircraft. We still maintain back-up drogue capability on the boom of the KC-10, our most modern tanker aircraft, because if the situation demands it, you can "scab" an exterior probe on a fighter easily—plumb it into its centerpoint refueling system. Flying-boom refueling gives unlimited range to our airplanes—fighters, bombers, cargo, reconnaissance, even the tankers themselves. The KC-10 can be refueled in the air before transferring fuel to a receiver.

Significant technological change has occurred in ejection systems. During my flight training days, pilots simply wore a parachute. If something happened, you jumped out and free-fell away from the airplane. When you fell to an altitude where you didn't need oxygen, you pulled the D-ring, and the chute opened. In some cases we were equipped with small bail-out oxygen bottles. If you jumped out of the airplane at high altitudes, you pulled the "apple"—the little ball that opened the valve—and let oxygen flow into your mouth or your mask while you were free-falling. Those bottles gave you about a ten-minute source of oxygen.

In the P-59s and P-80s, pilots were still equipped with parachutes. But we found that if the pilot had to jump at high speed, he would hit the side of the airplane or be blown into the tail. Usually that knocked him unconscious or killed him. We realized that we had to come up with a system to protect pilots and crews in the event that they had to bail out at jet speeds.

Ejection seats were developed in the late '40s, and by the early '50s, they were standard equipment in most jet aircraft. The pilot pulled a lever on his seat that released the canopy and the canopy was blown away. Then a cartridge charge—usually 57mm—blew the pilot seat clear of the airplane. When you were clear, you had to reach down and unhook your lap belt, fall free of the seat, and open your parachute manually. Then we refined the system, hooking the parachute D-ring to the seat, and added automatic timers. Two seconds after you ejected from the aircraft, the lap belt automatically opened, and the seat dropped away, pulling the D-ring to deploy the parachute.

It just so happens that some pilots have to bail out of airplanes at high altitude. With automatic timers deploying the parachute, we ran the risk of a guy freezing to death or running out of oxygen at high altitude. So we installed an aneroid cell in the system. When the pilot left the seat, the aneroid cell in the parachute was armed by the D-ring. The cell monitored atmospheric pressure, opening the chute only after the pilot fell below 14,000 feet. That eliminated the risk of the pilot freezing or running out of oxygen.

But we ran into other problems. With the F-104, a Mach 2 airplane, we found that if the pilot bailed out at high speeds, the cartridge charge wasn't capable of blowing the ejection seat above the tail of the aircraft. We went to a downward ejection system—the seat ejected through the floor of the airplane. That was the system in the early F-104s and the X-3. Obviously, downward ejection brought another problem. If the pilot was forced to bail out at low altitude and slow speed, then he had very little time to separate from the seat and deploy his parachute.

That led us to develop the ejection systems that are used in high-speed aircraft today—rocket seats. We went back to upward trajectory. Small solid-rocket motors boost the pilot clear of the airplane. We are now able to get the pilot safely out of the airplane, whether at zero speed and zero altitude or at high speed and high altitude. In the most advanced ejection seats, the pilot can bail out "on the deck"—at 300 feet of altitude—from an inverted aircraft doing 600 mph. That seat, using stabilizers and gyro sensors, will do a 180-degree turn and direct its trajectory upward. These systems are very reliable—a high percentage of pilots who eject today do so without injury.

Jet aviation also led to the development of sophisticated life support systems—oxygen masks and pressure suits. In the old days, when we were flying around below 12,000 feet, we didn't need to augment the air we breathed. But when you put a pilot at 18,000 feet, the atmospheric pressure is only one-half what it is at sea level, so he gets only one-half the oxygen in his blood stream that he would normally. You must augment the air he breathes with oxygen and increase the oxygen content as you go higher. At 33,000 feet, the atmospheric pressure is about one-fifth of sea-level pressure. A pilot at that altitude must breathe pure oxygen in order to absorb it in his blood stream and function normally.

As we went higher than 33,000 feet, we found that we had to pressurize the oxygen in the pilot's lungs to force it into the blood stream. We developed automatic oxygen regulators for unpressurized airplanes—as you went to higher altitudes, oxygen began blowing into your face mask. You would "pressure-breathe," forcing oxygen into your blood stream. When you get up to 43,000 or 44,000 feet, however, the pressure that is necessary to force oxygen into the blood stream approaches the mechanical and structural capabilities of your rib cage and lungs. Pressurized oxygen literally begins to blow you up.

Back in the '40s, we began to develop a device to support the rib cage—the "partial-pressure suit." I was instrumental in developing those pressure suits at Wright Field in the aeromedical laboratory pressure chambers. We were working on the old "Dr. Henry" suit—it was named for the physician who was developing it—and I wore it many times in pressure chambers in 1945 and 1946. It came out under the nomenclature, the "T-1 partial-pressure suit" or the "capstan" suit, and was available to me in 1947 for the X-1 program. I used that partial-pressure suit anytime I was operating the X-1 above 50,000 feet. It saved my life a few times.

We found, however, that the T-1 partial-pressure suit could not keep a pilot alive in a complete vacuum. We then went to a "full-pressure suit." Very basically—you fill a suit with air to an equivalent altitude pressure of about 35,000 feet and put the pilot inside that artificial atmosphere. The suit is a little stiff; it's not as mobile as the old "Dr. Henry" suit, but it's much more effective. It is life-sustaining in a complete vacuum. Those suits haven't changed much in 20 years. I was flying an SR-71 in August 1983 wearing a full-pressure suit similar to the pressure suit I was wearing back in 1963 when I flew the NF-104 above 100,000 feet. These same suits have been adapted by the NASA people for space missions.

I've flown with foreign air forces, pilots in all parts of the world—British, French, Pakistani, Iranian, Japanese, Chinese. There's an observation that I've made over many years of flying with many nationalities. There is no such thing as a natural-born pilot. I don't care what color he is or what his political or religious beliefs are, a pilot's capability is commensurate with his experience. The more experience he has, the better he is. It's that simple. That's the reason it's necessary to generate a sufficient amount of flying time in any outfit—and that's true in cargo, bomber, fighter, helicopter, or flight training.

And there's something that I've observed in the people of the United States Air Force. When I enlisted in World War II, every guy who flew or fought—at least, the guys that I knew—fought because it was his job. They were dedicated. Military guys don't make policy. They enforce it. If you're in Vietnam fighting, or in Korea fighting, or in Europe fighting in WWI or WWII, you're doing it because it's your job. As a squadron commander in the '50s, I recall being stationed in foreign countries, standing on alert with nuclear weapons hung on our fighters. Some of our targets were so far away that after we delivered weapons, we had enough fuel to get to a mountainous area and bail out. One-way mission. I never saw a pilot who questioned the orders that were given to him under those conditions. All the people in the Air Force—administrative people, training people, intelligence people, ground crews, pilots—understand that regardless of their individual missions, the Air Force is not going to be successful unless all functional areas work together. And their loyalty and dedication haven't changed, in my opinion, from the day I won my wings right on through today.

Chuck Yeager
B/Gen USAF Ret.

—Chuck Yeager

TACTICAL.

The F-16 can withstand up to nine Gs—nine times the force of gravity—with internal fuel tanks filled. No other fighter aircraft can match that capability. Special design features enhance the pilot's ability to withstand those extreme G forces. The seat-back angle was changed from the usual 13 degrees to 30 degrees and the heel rest is higher than normal, placing the pilot's feet closer to the level of his head. In this position the pilot is less likely to lose awareness when "pulling Gs." The pilot maintains excellent flight control of the F-16 through its "fly-by-wire" system. Electrical wires replace the usual cables and mechanical linkage controls. A side-stick is used instead of the conventional center-mounted stick. The pilot places his arm in a support rest and, with hand pressure and motion, sends electrical signals to the aileron, rudder, and other flight control surfaces. Pilots call the F-16 "the Electric Jet."

There's a popular misconception that flying a modern aircraft is difficult and dangerous. It isn't. Flying an airplane like the Eagle —getting it off a runway, cruising around, landing it—is the easiest thing in the world. Automated systems make elements of flying that were once difficult quite simple today, and safety records for jet aircraft bear that out—they've improved year after year.

"The difficult part is 'employing' the aircraft, that is, getting it to destroy other aircraft, reaching its performance potential. Only a very small number of people are able to do that well. No matter what your physical or intellectual abilities, you don't just walk out of a college classroom and take an F-15 fighter to its performance peak. You have to be trained. A four-G turn is an elevator ride in these planes—it's nothing unusual. Turns of six Gs aren't unusual. An F-16 can pull nine Gs—nine times the force of gravity.

"That makes it incredibly physically demanding to fly in a dogfight. You come back from a mission soaked with perspiration. Pilots wear something called a G-suit, which is an inflatable bladder that automatically squeezes your lower body as you execute a turn, helping to keep the blood in the upper part of your body. You train yourself to lock your leg muscles and tighten your stomach muscles to help keep the blood in your head. There's so much pressure on your diaphragm that you can only draw short gasps of air, so you're grunting. If you listen to cockpit tapes of a dogfight, it sounds like a wrestling match.

"In an air-to-air engagement, you almost never look directly out the front of the cockpit. You do that only a moment before you destroy your target. You're usually looking out the top or side of the canopy. But with six or more Gs working on you, it's incredibly difficult just to hold your head up to do that. Visual contact in an air-to-air engagement is crucial. At the speeds we fly, a hostile aircraft a mile away is close-range, but it looks like a dot. There's a saying among fighter pilots that a fool and his target are soon parted. So you never take your eyes off him. Your ears are full of radio talk. You don't think of the mechanics of flying at all, you just think of the objective. You don't look at airspeed, but you can always feel how fast you're going by the way the plane responds to you.

"The F-4 Phantom is not a delicate, agile machine like an F-15. Some guys call the F-4 'Double Ugly.' Or they call it the 'Rhino.' That's because it's a very tough airplane and can take a lot of damage. Pilots of the F-4 are very straightforward in combat. The F-4 is good both air-to-air and air-to-ground, so pilots will often shoot their way through a dogfight on their way to a bombing mission. The F-4 is a real workhorse. We have two-man crews. The pilot sits in the front seat of the cockpit. The GIB, the guy in back, is the weapons system operator, WSO, or 'Whizzo.'

"There's real satisfaction in flying. You get immediate feedback—you do something and the aircraft responds to it. It's immediate, hands-on job satisfaction."

—*an F-15 pilot*

"Checking six" is the term fighter pilots use to indicate looking to the rear of the aircraft, the area most vulnerable to attack. The cockpit area is divided into quadrants for quick location of other aircraft. Directly forward is 12 o'clock, to the left is nine o'clock, and to the right is three o'clock.

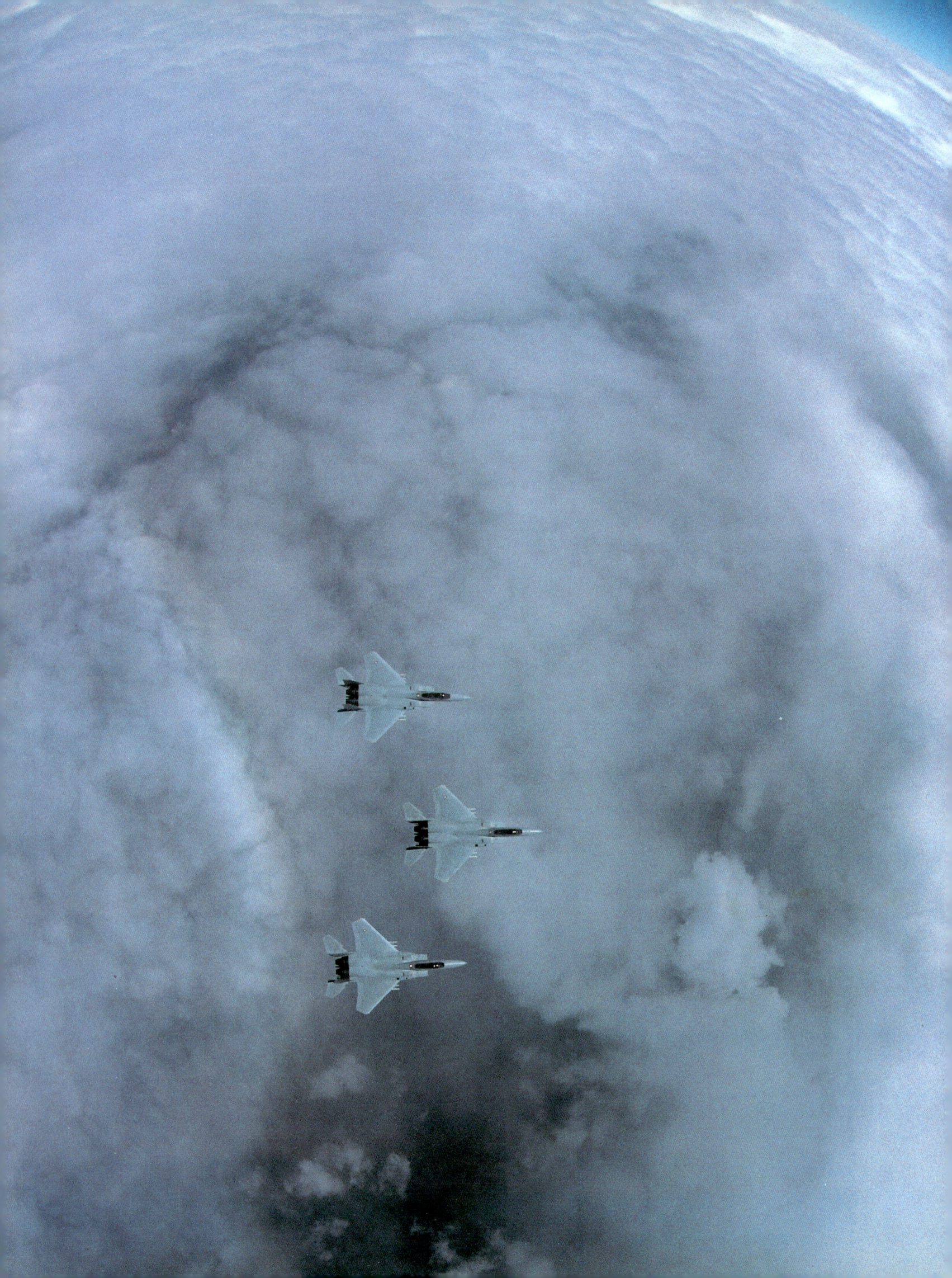

The F-15 Eagle is the first Air Force operational aircraft whose engines' thrust exceeds the plane's loaded weight, making it possible for the Eagle to accelerate even in a vertical climb. With its low wing-loading (a low ratio of aircraft weight to wing surface) and thrust-to-weight ratio, the aircraft can turn tightly without losing airspeed. Six of the eight world time-to-height records are held by the F-15A, Project Streak Eagle. The Streak Eagle climbed to an altitude of 65,616 feet in 2 minutes, 2.94 seconds.

"Since I had flown the F-4 Phantom for eight years, I was skeptical when I joined the first operational wing of A-10s. Public affairs people may call them Thunderbolts, but no flier does. We call them 'Hogs.' They aren't sleek and they aren't fast. But I developed real respect for the airplane. It's designed specifically for close-air support, a tough machine built to operate in a 'high-threat environment' —where the fronts of two opposing armies meet.

"It is critically important in that situation to maintain a full perspective of the battlefield. You can't do that in an F-4. At 450 knots, all you see are the big things—rivers, trees, rail lines. But at the speed and altitude the Hog flies, you can see troops hiding in a clump of trees, can cue on where the guns of a helicopter gunship below you are pointed, can see aspects of terrain you would never have time to notice in another fighter.

"There's smoke and dust and confusion beneath you. You've got to come in underneath artillery fire the opposing fronts are sending toward each other. There's ground fire everywhere—small arms fire, anti-aircraft fire, mortars, hand-held rockets. For a fighter pilot, it's a new way of thinking. You can't use your speed to get out of trouble. You have to use your ingenuity; learn to use terrain as a defense for your aircraft, 'pop up' or 'unmask,' that is, bring the aircraft out from wherever you're concealing it, deliver ordnance or fire on your target, and survive. You have to think through a whole new set of tactics.

"Something else that's different in the Hog is the 30mm cannon mounted in the nose—specifically designed to be an anti-tank, armor-penetrating weapon. Most guns on fighters are 20mm. The 30mm cannon is incredible—it has such a long range and generates so much energy. Although you don't experience that much vibration or noise when you fire, an automatic pitch compensator trims the nose lift from the recoil. The cannon is a highly accurate air-to-surface weapon at ranges up to 4,000 or even 6,000 feet—over a mile.

"Some people say that because the A-10 is not a high-speed aircraft it won't survive, that it's too exposed. But in close-air support, regardless of the speed of your aircraft, there comes a moment when you must expose yourself, when you must be willing to risk your aircraft and your life to complete your mission. Reading a map, navigating at 240 knots by church steeples and roads—in many ways the A-10 is one of the last bastions of the old stick-and-rudder school.

"A point we make with the guys who are flying the F-15s and 16s, whipping around and practicing for air-to-air engagement, is that they can go up and knock everything out of the sky and have their whole squadron made up of aces. But it won't matter when they fly back to base and there's an enemy tank along with a truckload of troops sitting next to their hangars. Say what you will, it's the 'grunts,' the men on the ground, who win the war. That's why I take pride in being a 'Hog-driver.' We help the grunts. Someone's got to go down there and grovel in the mud to win, and that's what a Hog does best."

—*an A-10 pilot*

STRATEGIC

I've flown ten different aircraft. Flying the 'BUFF' has been my most challenging and rewarding experience. The B-52 aircraft commander is responsible for getting six people to work together with a single mind and a single purpose for a nine-hour mission. There's no place to move around in the airplane, and each crewman has a specific responsibility every step of the mission. The pilot and copilot sit side-by-side in the cockpit and must anticipate each other's every move. Two hundred twenty-five tons with eight engines—that's a lot of airplane to manage. 'Down in the hole,' beneath the pilot deck, are the navigator and radar-navigator. They are responsible for providing long-range navigation information and delivering ordnance over a target. There are no windows down there, just radar screens and controls. In the back of the plane are two more crewmen. They are responsible for the air defenses, the protection of the aircraft. All these people have to work together to point that big, ugly, fat thing down two miles—two miles!—of runway, get airborne, find a tanker circling in the sky out over nowhere and hook up with it, shut down navigation and communications systems for training and security, deliver ordnance, test air defenses, and get safely home.

"The B-52 is an aircraft of total anticipation. It's so big, you must know how it will respond to a maneuver in order to compensate before the initial control has taken effect. That can get tricky at low altitude. The BUFF was designed for high-altitude missions. The role of the aircraft was expanded when surface-to-air defenses changed. We have to be able to bring it in under radar. When you've got the BUFF down at 300 feet, traveling at six miles a minute in turbulence, you really get shaken around. There's quite a bit of wing flex—about 13 feet at each wing tip. You can see the wings flapping out there. But the B-52 will take a beating. That's been proved in combat, and there was a famous test flight conducted when the plane's low-level capability was being developed. A test crew was flying at low altitude, trying to find turbulence, to see how the plane would perform. They found turbulence all right, so much that the tail of the plane was ripped off. They were able to bring the aircraft back and land it safely. That's durability.

"The plane has an unusual feature in landing. Usually when an aircraft lands in a crosswind, the pilot dips a wing slightly to compensate. That's risky with a B-52, because of the length of the wings. It's easy to catch a wing tip or an engine. So the B-52 is designed to be 'crabbed' on landing. The plane has bicycle landing gear under the fuselage that can be steered. Rather than dip a wing, a BUFF pilot turns the aircraft nose into the crosswind, then adjusts for the angle by steering the landing gear so the wheels point straight down the runway. It's like a great big green crab walking sideways.

"Among fliers there's a term called 'air sense.' It means a person has good judgment, has the ability to make decisions quickly. Good air sense is the key to becoming a B-52 pilot."

—*a B-52 pilot*

Because of the sweep of its wings, the center of lift for a B-52 is behind its center of gravity. Unlike most jet aircraft, which climb to altitude and land nose up, the B-52 lands and climbs slightly nose down. Its eight engines have no afterburners. Additional thrust is provided by a water injection system that makes the B-52's takeoff a deafening roar.

When the instructor takes you out in the T-38 for training, you go to altitude and take it to Mach 1. I remember thinking, 'So this is it? Going faster than the speed of sound, this is no big deal.' Up there, you have no visual references, not even clouds. But going supersonic 'on the deck,' that is, at treetop level, is an incredible experience. It's a blur.

"The FB-111 can fly all day long on the deck. It's so quiet and stable, it feels like a Cadillac. It is the premier, low-level, high-speed, all-weather penetrator. With its Terrain-Following Radar, you can fly the FB-111 hands off on the deck, day or night. TFR enables you to fly as low as 200 feet at 1.2 Mach. Instruments give you information on the terrain, and a beeper tells you when you are starting a climb or descent. It's amazing equipment. New guys in the FB-111 can find it a little disconcerting to drop 10,000 to 12,000 feet a minute after crossing a mountain peak at night. But you learn how to monitor the controls so you can trust the system.

"There are two on-board computers in the FB-111. With its automatic systems, it's possible to load an entire mission reel-to-reel. All the pilot has to do is indicate destination. The computer will give information on airspeed, which the pilot implements according to the required time of arrival, and the airplane flies itself there. You can then feed it another destination, and it will fly there, and so on through the course of a mission.

"At eye level in front of the pilot is the Optical Display Sight, the ODS, which gives information on the altitude of the aircraft, monitors airspeed, gives climb-dive commands for low-level TFR, and commands for instrument landings. In the center of the display is our bomb sight.

"On the nose of the aircraft is a disk called the 'Astro-tracker.' Even on bright, sunny days it can track stars for the astral navigation system. The navigator sits alongside the pilot in the cockpit. He serves as copilot, navigator, radar-navigator, that is, bombadier, and electronic warfare operator, providing the defensive capability of the aircraft.

"The purpose of the movable wings is to give the aircraft more maneuverability through a bigger performance envelope. The wings can be swept from 16 degrees to 72.5 degrees from perpendicular. Takeoffs and landings are normally done with the wings at 16 degrees. With the wings forward, slats and flaps enable the FB-111 to fly at quite slow airspeeds, making it possible to use shorter runways. The attitude of the wings for normal cruising is 26 degrees. The inside carrier pylons on the wings hinge to keep load drag to a minimum. Wing sweep must be carefully controlled for particular performance requirements. Certain maneuvers at certain speeds can overload the wings and cause loss of control. Pilots have to meet stiff flight experience requirements before they ever fly an FB-111.

"For supersonic flight the wings are swept back. I've flown the aircraft at Mach 2.1 at 50,000 feet. The plane is so quiet you don't even realize that you're whistling along up there. When you take it to speed we say you're going to 'sweep and smoke.' You smoke all right. Speed is one of the FB-111's defenses. If a fighter gets in behind you, you know that you can run faster for a greater distance than he can. You've got more gas. So you engage afterburn and smoke."

—*an FB-111 pilot*

Because the B-1B looks small and sleek in flight, people tend not to realize how big it is. The B-1B is about the same length as the B-52. When you stand next to it on the runway, there's no doubt in your mind that you're looking at a strategic bomber. Yet its design and systems make the radar cross section of the B-1 only a hundredth of the cross section of the B-52.

"Much of the technology of the F-111 has been refined in this aircraft. Like the F-111, the B-1B has movable wings—16 degrees full forward, 25 degrees for cruise, and 67.5 degrees maximum sweep for supersonic flight. We also have Terrain-Following Radar, which allows us to do 700 miles per hour on the deck. We've had eleven years experience flying TFR in the F-111. While 'jamming' was sometimes successful in the F-111's TFR in combat, it would be very difficult to jam the B-1's system. TFR doesn't put out much energy—it's like a pencil point, so it's very difficult to detect. We've also had considerable experience utilizing electronic countermeasures. An early model of the B-1 had a long spine on the fuselage that carried electronic equipment. We elected not to go with that particular package, so the long spine doesn't appear in our newer models. You'll notice areas of black coating on the leading edges of the wings—under it are antennas for electronic equipment. While there are no lethal countermeasures on the aircraft, it is extremely survivable.

"I've flown missions testing the electronics. Our job was to mask the aircraft behind a range of mountains, indicate our location, employ our countermeasures, then pop up and come in on the deck. Guys in a control tower were using equipment to detect us. Five times we came up over the mountains from the same direction, and five times they had us pegged before we could get to the tower. The sixth time I told them I was changing my approach, that I would be coming over the mountains to the north. A guy in the tower accidentally left the microphone on, and I could hear them shuffling papers and moving equipment all over the place. I radioed and told them to look out the tower window. We dipped a wing as we flew over. Then I told them we were coming in again from a different direction. We came in from the south up a riverbed and dipped a wing to them as we flew over again. It's significant that those guys in the tower had optimum conditions—they were Ph.D.s, had the best of equipment, coffee and doughnuts, and plenty of help, yet when we simulated actual conditions they couldn't find us. In the real thing, controllers will be out in the field somewhere, understaffed, probably with effective communications knocked out. The electronic countermeasures on the aircraft are the best in the world. With its speed and low-level capability, the B-1 is unstoppable.

"A percentage of the B-1 force will be kept 'cocked on alert.' The aircraft has specially designed systems to get it off the ground quickly. If the alarm sounds, the crews either run or drive in cars out to 'alert trees,' where the planes are kept on branching lanes by the runway. There is a special button on the nose gear of the aircraft. Any crew member can activate it. When the button is pushed, the ladder to the cockpit immediately descends, and the auxiliary power units start up. By the time the pilot gets in the cockpit, he can throw a couple of switches, and the engines are up to speed. We can taxi to takeoff in moments.

"The B-1 is our first strategic bomber to have afterburners. Afterburner doubles the thrust of each engine from 15,000 pounds to 30,000 pounds. With a takeoff weight of 360,000 pounds, we can get the aircraft airborne in 6,000 feet. That makes it possible for the B-1 to operate out of a number of airfields where the B-52 can't."

(continued on page 75)

(continued from page 72)

"A great deal of 'human-factors engineering' went into the design of the B-1. Cockpit visibility is excellent because the windows are so big—it's easy to check for wing clearance when you're taxiing. The cockpit layout is great. Everything's in a consolidated package—electronics, hydraulics, fuel monitors. Both the pilot and copilot have stick, throttles, and wing sweep handle, and both have a full set of instruments. The Offensive Systems Operator and the Defensive Systems Operator sit behind a bulkhead to the rear of the cockpit. Like the pilot and copilot, they face forward in the aircraft. We communicate with them by interphone.

"The canards, the small flaps on the front of the aircraft, bang like crazy in flight. The center of gravity in the B-1 is 50 feet to the rear of the cockpit, which makes for a large angle of moment. Where the wings move one foot in turbulence, the cockpit area might move ten feet. One mission I was asked to fly the aircraft manually with the canards off. There was a noticeable difference in air fatigue. The canards really smooth out the ride.

"When you're flying the B-1B, you don't have the feeling of size at all. The wings are designed so that when they are swept, there is only one square foot less surface than when the wings are forward—at low level, the plane surprises you with its maneuverability. Many pilots will tell you that the B-1 handles like a fighter."

—*a B-1B pilot*

AIRLIFT/TANKER

"When I graduated from flight training class I had my choice of commands. I selected airlift because I was fascinated with the idea of traveling all over the world. The C-141 is Marco Polo's dream. It flies everywhere. And it gives you an opportunity to be your own boss—as flight commander, you're responsible for keeping the mission moving, no matter in what out-of-the-way place you pick up or deliver cargo.

"When you're on the ground, it's like managing a three-ring circus. You're unloading so much cargo, making sure it's being distributed properly, there's so much fuel to take on, miles of hydraulic and electrical line running everywhere, and 15 or 20 crew members to look after. I think the whole complicated process must be what it was like when they brought the old sailing ships into port.

"Airlift pilots are trained to fly smooth, to find the middle of the performance envelope and stay in it. That makes takeoff and landing a real challenge. The C-5 is a massive airplane. It weighs three-quarters of a million pounds. To 'grease one on'—land smooth—takes skill. The C-5 is designed to withstand more than three Gs. But we don't teach airlift pilots to pull Gs. We teach them energy management.

"There's a macho image associated with flying the C-130 Hercules, or 'Herky Bird.' It's an all-purpose aircraft that's been around for a long time and seen some heavy action. At least two C-130 pilots are Medal of Honor winners. The Hercules is ideal for short-field operations. It torques up fast and slows down quickly. Its props work great for dirt field landings because they don't suck up debris like jet engines.

"Airlift guys are called 'trash haulers.' But that 'trash' is essential equipment. Without airlift, ground and air forces can't do their jobs—they can't even get to their jobs. We provide strategic and tactical mobility for American military forces. And we're proud of the fact that we provide earthquake, famine, flood relief, and diplomatic assistance in peacetime. The airlift system is a worldwide lifeline—both in peace and in war. My longest flight was nearly 20 hours. It's not particularly exciting to sit up there at cruise altitude, drilling a hole in the sky. But you know you always have people depending on you, whether it's airborne troops ready to drop out the rear, or people on the ground who need medicine and food."

—a C-141 pilot

The C-141 Starlifter is the first jet aircraft designed specifically to meet military airlift needs. Carrying a maximum of 123 fully equipped paratroops, it can deliver them, along with equipment and supplies, either by landing or by airdrop, using two paratroop doors on each side of the aircraft and a rear loading ramp.

Built to provide massive strategic airlift for deployment and supply of combat and support forces, the C-5 Galaxy is nearly as long as a football field and as high as a six-story building. It can transport virtually any piece of U.S. Army combat equipment, including tanks, self-propelled artillery, helicopters, and the 74-ton mobile scissors bridge. The C-5 is the largest aircraft in the world.

"The boom operator, the 'boomer,' goes back to the 'boom pod' of the KC-135 for refueling. You lie stomach down on a pallet with your chin in a rest. It's not comfortable, and there's no heat back there, so it gets pretty cold. In front of you are the control panel gauges, and beyond that you look out the rear of the aircraft through a small window. The boom control stick is beneath the pallet on your right. We use the 'ruddevators,' the small wings on the boom, to fly the cone into the gas receptacle of the 'receiver,' the aircraft to be refueled.

"From the moment he is in the pod the boomer is responsible for the success of the mission. When you have two or more aircraft flying in close proximity like that, especially when any of the operators is inexperienced, there is potential for damage.

"We try to refuel at altitudes where there is a minimum of turbulence, but we sometimes hit bad weather. An F-16 fighter can surge so quickly that it can be back in position before the boomer has time to react. It's easy for those sudden movements to damage the boom icing shield. But fighters don't take much gas, so they refuel quickly. For a big 'wide-body' like the C-5, it's a different situation. The wide-bodies move slower, but they push a big wave of air in front of them. With a C-5 coming up behind you, you can feel the tail of the KC-135 start to lift. You have to fight the bow wave generated by the C-5 with the control stick of the boom and stay in contact for a longer period of time. Fatigue becomes a factor.

"The visual point of reference for the receiver is not the boom or the tail of the tanker. The receiver looks toward the fore section of the KC-135 fuselage. There are light panels on the belly of the tanker that are controlled by the boomer back in the pod. Those lights tell the receiver to go up or down, left or right. The boom can withstand bending and motion, but only to a point. There is an orange stripe painted down the centerline of the tanker to help the receiver monitor his azimuth, or lateral motion, to keep himself lined up with the tanker.

"A mission usually follows this procedure. There is an established ARCP, Aircraft Receiver Control Point, where the refueling is to take place. The tanker flies in and begins an orbital flight pattern. Ideally, the tanker rolls out right in front of the receivers as they arrive. The receivers must adjust their speed to come in approximately 50 feet aft and ten feet below the tanker and stabilize. The boomer then clears for contact position and flies the boom into position. Refueling receptacles vary. Some aircraft have 'slip-ways,' which make it easier to lay the nozzle down and slide it in. Others have pop-up receptacles. Some receptacles are located forward on the aircraft, others further back. When the boom is in position, the nozzle is telescoped out, contact is made, and we begin pumping gas. Once the refueling mission is completed, the boomer flies the boom up to the chock position on the tail of the tanker. There is a cable system to haul the boom up manually if necessary.

"Some of the pilots joke with us, call us 'gas passers.' But they know we're the guys who get them the fuel they need to complete a mission. In combat situations, disabled aircraft have even hooked up with a tanker and been towed far enough to come down over water or make it to an airfield. Receivers listen to what the boomer has to say."
—a KC-135 boom operator

Called "the Specter," the AC-130H is a heavily armed gunship. Its side-firing weapons are linked by computer with a highly sophisticated sensor system. Forward-looking infrared target acquisition equipment, low-light-level TV camera, and laser target designators give the Specter night operation capability. The gunship has a firepower capability of over 17,000 rounds per minute.

SPECIAL SYSTEMS

The black paint serves two major purposes. First, it works as a 'heat sink,' that is, it draws off the extreme temperatures the SR-71 experiences and cools the aircraft through auxiliary systems. Second, radar works best on bright, shiny surfaces. Black paint dampens the radar reflection and makes the SR much harder to detect.

"Most people who fly the 'Blackbird' have flown tactical airplanes. But it's not a physical airplane like a fighter where you're physically engaged in flying it—ripping around the sky and pulling Gs. This is more of a cerebral airplane. You call upon your entire experience to ensure that the airplane is doing precisely what it's supposed to. With such extremes of temperature and speed, we're still finding engineering things that aren't in the textbooks.

"When you're flying at Mach 3 above 70,000 feet, you're walking a very thin line in terms of the airplane's performance. Over a 'take' area, that part of the mission when the reconnaissance system is in operation, the computerized automatic pilot flies the aircraft. No human could operate the SR smoothly enough and long enough for the cameras to work to their full capability. But you have to be ready to intercede at any moment in an all-or-nothing fashion. Subsonic, the SR-71 handles like a fighter. It's stable, handles great. But supersonic, it can get you into trouble.

"Any aircraft that goes supersonic creates a shock wave. You cannot allow a shock wave to pass through a jet engine or it will 'flame out,' that is, stop burning. The SR-71 rides on a shock wave when it is at speed. You can see the wave move back along the aircraft. The 'spikes'—cones in the engine intake ducts—control the air that flows into the engines, and a computerized duct system controls the air that flows out, providing a way to manage the shock wave right at the threshold of the intakes. If the shock wave starts moving back into an engine, the computer will move the spike forward and shut the intake. It will not reopen until the air has been expelled through the ducts. When an intake shuts, it causes an extreme yaw in the attitude of the aircraft, so violent it slams your helmet against the side of the cockpit. That's an 'unstart' or 'AD'—aerodynamic disturbance.

"An experienced pilot can anticipate it. You can hear something called 'duct rumble.' When you hear it, you know that you need to intercede, that the shock wave is moving too far back. You're in a hostile environment on a number of counts. At speed, temperatures get up to 500 degrees inside the aircraft and up to 1,200 degrees at the tailpipe. On re-entry, temperatures outside can drop to −65 degrees. You're inside a pressure suit. That's to save your life. Your blood will boil in the atmosphere at 60,000 feet; at 70,000 feet your blood will evaporate. You're usually over a geographic area where the last thing you can allow to happen is a flame-out. You have to monitor your fuel consumption all the time, make sure you're drawing from appropriate tanks to control the center of gravity of the aircraft. The computer does that, but the computer doesn't always work. Missions I've flown have lasted anywhere from 57 minutes to ten hours. Squeeze tubes are your only source of food and drink. It's a challenge. Everybody's watching you—other pilots because the plane is so exotic, generals because its missions are so sensitive. You're completely drained. I've never slept so well as when I've returned from a mission."

(continued on page 113)

(continued from page 108)

"The engines are tremendously powerful. Since you're in the pressure suit, you don't hear a thing. But for someone standing on the ground, the afterburners make your insides vibrate. It feels like your teeth might shatter. When you select afterburners to go to speed, you really get a kick in the seat of the pants. The prettiest sight I've ever seen in my life was in the SR-71. There's a periscope in the cockpit that you can flip up. It gives you a look aft at the engines and stabilizers. One morning about two a.m., I put the SR in a slight bank, turned up the power, and looked back through the periscope. The sky was pitch black, and against it you could see the concentric rings of a shock wave going back from the engines, and then the afterburners came to points and grew longer and longer, perfect blue, a perfect plume. It was beautiful."

—*an SR-71 pilot*

The SR-71, called "the Blackbird," flies at three times the speed of sound, faster than the muzzle velocity of a 30.06 bullet, at the borders of outer space. Even in the thin atmosphere of that altitude, its titanium skin heats so much that the aircraft grows in length from six inches to a foot. No sealant has been developed that can withstand the extremes of temperature the aircraft experiences in flight and re-entry, so the SR-71 leaks fuel badly on the runway and is usually refueled right after takeoff. A strategic reconnaissance aircraft, it is unarmed. Its defenses are altitude and speed.

The U-2 has center trucks under the fuselage for landing gear—so it's like a bicycle on takeoff and landing. There are rollers mounted in the middle of each wing called 'pogos,' like training wheels on a bike. The ground crew takes the pins out of the pogos prior to takeoff. When you engage power, you have time for a quick look at your instruments, then you must concentrate on what's going on outside. With all that surface, the wings start to fly as soon as you accelerate. When the wings lift, the pogos drop away. It's not unusual for that to happen within 15 or 20 feet after you release brakes. It takes 2,000 to 3,000 feet to get the U-2 airborne, so from the moment you release the brakes—even though you're still on the runway—you are flying the aircraft. You have to concentrate on keeping those long wings level, using ailerons to compensate for any crosswind. It's a problem for some people who train for U-2. I've seen guys with excellent flight backgrounds in other aircraft come in and not even be able to get the U-2 off the runway.

"Landing presents special problems, too. As you start your approach, you monitor the amount of fuel in your tanks, which are located in each wing, and pump fuel to balance the load. If there's no crosswind, and the fuel load is balanced, you can come in, land, and keep upright. I think in all my missions in the U-2, I've managed to do that five times. Usually what happens is that the wings are slightly unbalanced, or wind blows you over, so you drag a wing. There are titanium skids for protection on each wing tip. Then guys we call 'wing walkers' hustle out to the plane, and pull down the up wing. It can be tough. Baffles in the fuel tanks slow down the flow, but all your gas starts running to one end of the wing. Once they've got you upright, they walk you to wherever you park the aircraft.

"The whole process probably looks strange to someone not involved in flying the U-2, but we go through it because everything possible is done to cut weight for maximum fuel economy. When you're 'loitering,' flying in pattern over your station, it's essential that you be able to stay up there for a long time. Sometimes you have to wait for clouds to break so you can photograph.

"Missions are usually long-duration sorties in excess of nine hours. The pilot shows up three hours prior to takeoff and has a basic physical exam by a med tech or flight surgeon. Then we eat a high-protein, low-residue breakfast, usually steak and eggs. This is about all the food the pilot gets for the next 13 hours, although you can eat 'tube food' through your helmet flap—the applesauce isn't bad, but most guys stick to water and Gatorade.

"After breakfast, technicians help the pilot suit up. It's like wearing a rubber bag—it's hot and heavy. You carry your own portable air-conditioning system—it looks like a metal briefcase. After suit-up everyone goes out of his way to minimize the pilot's exertion. People pick up things for you; another pilot even 'pre-flights' the aircraft for you. All the switches in the cockpit are set when you go out.

"The med techs have you breathe pure oxygen for one hour. This purges your body of nitrogen to prevent bends. Technicians then perform 'integration,' that is, they strap you in the cockpit. Unlike the SR-71, where you're strapped in for an hour before takeoff to check out all the automated systems, we start engines and taxi out right away. It's usually just ten minutes from integration to takeoff."

—*a U-2 pilot*

A completely operational AWACS aircraft costs approximately $140 million. That's a lot of responsibility. Most AWACS pilots come from the 'heavies,' that is, we have experience flying aircraft with no less than four engines, and all of us have a tremendous amount of flight time. To qualify as a copilot for AWACS, you must have a minimum of 1,200 hours flying time; for pilot, a minimum of 2,000 hours. You must have established a very high level of flight competency before you ever take the controls.

"The AWACS is fun to fly. It has tremendously powerful engines and is highly maneuverable. We go everywhere. If a foreign country places a telephone call to the Pentagon, we can have an AWACS there in 24 hours. Anyplace in the world. So we see extended TDY—temporary duty—in some remote places. I've seen quite a bit of time in Iceland, Egypt, Saudi Arabia, Khartoum, and Korea.

"Because its structure is unique, the aircraft is highly visible in other countries. People are fascinated by it. The AWACS has become an adaptation of Teddy Roosevelt's concept of 'the Great White Fleet.' He envisioned sending Navy gunships to any part of the world where we needed to make the American presence felt. Now we do it with AWACS. Pilots and crew have to function as diplomats as well as crew members.

"We consistently operate at altitudes higher than 29,000 feet. A typical mission lasts from 14 to 18 hours. This gives us tremendous eye-in-the-sky and communications capability. With a good AWACS crew and supplemental ground radar, we can detect and track almost anything as soon as its wheels leave a runway, and anything airborne beyond the horizon. It is extremely important that we keep other aircraft away from us when we are on a mission, not so much for our safety as for theirs. Emissions from the Rotodome—the radar dish—can cause fuel explosions, saturate the human body, and trigger electronic munitions.

"While the AWACS has no active defense systems, it is mobile and extremely survivable. Its reconnaissance and surveillance capabilities give it a force-multiplier effect achieved by no other aircraft."
—*an E-3A pilot*

The E-3A Sentry Airborne Warning and Control System, AWACS, carries highly sophisticated radar and communications equipment and an average crew of 14 members. The top of the fuselage is lined with lead to protect crew members from the powerful emissions of the Rotodome, the radar dish that rotates when the system is in operation. On-board air control systems can be used to direct friendly aircraft into intercept positions. While the Rotodome causes some loss of airspeed, its shape actually enhances lift.

A modified Boeing 747 jet transport, the E-4A/B is used by the Joint Chiefs of Staff as the National Emergency Airborne Command Post, NEACP. In the event of a national emergency or the destruction of United States ground command centers, NEACP provides a survivable means of carrying out the war orders of the National Command Authorities. The E-4B also performs the Strategic Air Command Airborne Command Post mission. The aircraft has worldwide communications capability through tactical satellite systems and carries airborne launch equipment for the Minuteman missile force. NEACP and a SAC Airborne Command Post are in the sky somewhere in the world 24 hours a day, seven days a week.

People have asked how I made the pictures for WINGS. There were a number of factors. I was privileged to fly with some of the finest pilots in the United States Air Force. I used film and equipment that proved absolutely dependable for the one-time opportunities that you find in air-to-air photography. And there was the professional, dedicated work of Air Force personnel. Hundreds of individuals are involved before I ever get to look out a boomer's window to see a B-1, F-16, or C-5 sliding up into pre-contact position. Air Force public affairs people in Washington, administrative and scheduling people at the major commands and out at the wings, maintenance crews, training officers, operations people—everyone involved, from the 19-year-old ground crewman to the seasoned wing commander with thousands of flight hours in his logbook, contributed to the success of these pictures.

I use Leica cameras and Kodachrome film. Leicas just seem to fit my hands—my grandmother gave me my first one, a Leica M3 with a 50mm lens, when I was a student at Rochester Institute of Technology. I still have that camera. I continued to use Leicas as a Navy photojournalist. Today, when I travel on assignment for TIME MAGAZINE, I pack my trusty Leica range-finder cameras as well as Leica's newest reflex, the R4. A little over half the pictures in WINGS were made with Leicaflex SL2 cameras; the rest were made with R4s. Except for one or two frames, the photographs in WINGS were made on Kodachrome 64.

Between the subject and the film comes the lens. For me, Leitz provides the perfect balance between image sharpness and image contrast. The lenses I use have been rebuilt so many times and are so battered that they look ready for retirement. I am constantly amazed, leaning over the light tables at TIME, with the quality they produce assignment after assignment.

I made a number of changes in my equipment to adapt it for air-to-air photography. My lenses have very light lubricants for quick focusing. Several of my camera bodies are modified so that the shutter will operate in a high-G environment—most cameras are designed to operate in a one-G world, not the world of jet fighters. I also have some long lenses in rapid-focusing mounts for ground photography.

In addition to the people of the United States Air Force, I must thank Steve Smith and Walter Heun at Leitz, Rockleigh, for making sure I always had cameras and sound advice during the production of WINGS. Also, Ken Hansen and his staff provided invaluable input during the final months of shooting. If it was a Leica, Ken had it. My special thanks to Arnold Drapkin, the picture editor at TIME MAGAZINE, for giving me the time and encouragement to complete WINGS.

—*Mark Meyer*

F-4

USAF designation: F-4 Phantom II
Nickname: Double Ugly, Wild Weasel, Rhino

The F-4 Phantom II is a twin-engine, all-weather, tactical fighter-bomber capable of speeds of more than 1,600 mph and altitudes approaching 60,000 feet. Flight speeds of 150 to 165 mph, necessary for short landing field operations, are made possible by the use of high-lift flaps. All F-4 models have folding wings for easy aircraft storage and ground handling.

The Air Force flew its first F-4 in May 1963. The F-4C, called the Wild Weasel, is a Navy F-4B model modified to meet Air Force requirements. Changes include wider-tread, low-pressure tires; larger wheels and brakes; cartridge starters; dual controls; boom in-flight refueling; and an inertial navigation system. The F-4C has a pod-mounted 20mm multibarrel gun and outer mountings for a large weapon load.

The Phantom F-4D model features major changes that increase accuracy in weapons delivery. The Air Force received its first F-4D in March 1966.

The first F-4E was delivered in October 1967. This model has an additional fuselage fuel tank, leading-edge slats for increased maneuverability, an improved engine, and an internally mounted 20mm multibarrel gun with improved fire-control system.

F-4Es were first fitted with target-identification systems in 1973. Essentially a television camera with zoom lens, each system provides long-range visual identification of airborne or ground targets. Modified systems provide the F-4E with day-night, all-weather capability to acquire, track, and designate ground targets for laser, infrared, and electro-optically guided weapons.

The F-4G Wild Weasel models, first delivered to the Air Force in 1978, increase the survivability of tactical strike forces by seeking out and suppressing or destroying enemy radar-directed anti-aircraft batteries and surface-to-air missile sites. The F-4G is equipped with sophisticated electronic warfare equipment in place of the internally mounted 20mm gun of the F-4E and can carry a greater variety of weapons than earlier Wild Weasel aircraft.

There are more than 1,000 F-4 Phantoms in the Air Force inventory. They are assigned to the Tactical Air Command, United States Air Forces in Europe, Pacific Air Forces, Alaskan Air Command, Air National Guard, and Air Force Reserve.

Primary function: all-weather tactical fighter-bomber
Prime contractor: McDonnell Aircraft Co., McDonnell Douglas Corp.
Power plant/manufacturer: two General Electric turbojet engines with afterburners: F-4C/D—J79-GE-15, F-4E/G—J79-GE-17
Thrust: each engine with afterburner: F-4C/D—17,000 pounds, F-4E/G—17,900 pounds
Dimensions: wingspan 38 feet 11 inches; length F-4C/D—58 feet 3 inches, F-4E/G—62 feet 11 inches; height 16 feet 5 inches
Speed: more than Mach 2 at 40,000 feet
Ceiling: above 60,000 feet
Range: beyond 1,300 miles with typical tactical load
Crew: two—pilot and weapons systems operator
Armament: F-4C/D—four AIM-7E Sparrow and four AIM-9 Sidewinder missiles, provisions for 20mm gun pods at fuselage centerline station or outboard pylons, and one fuselage centerline bomb rack and four pylon bomb racks capable of carrying up to 12,500 pounds of general purpose bombs; nuclear weapon capability; F-4E—one 20mm M61A-1 multibarrel gun, four AIM-7 Sparrow and four AIM-9 Sidewinder missiles, and one fuselage centerline bomb rack and four pylon bomb racks capable of carrying 12,500 pounds of general purpose bombs; F-4G—same as F-4E except gun removed and Shrike, standard ARM and HARM capability added
Maximum takeoff weight: 58,000 pounds

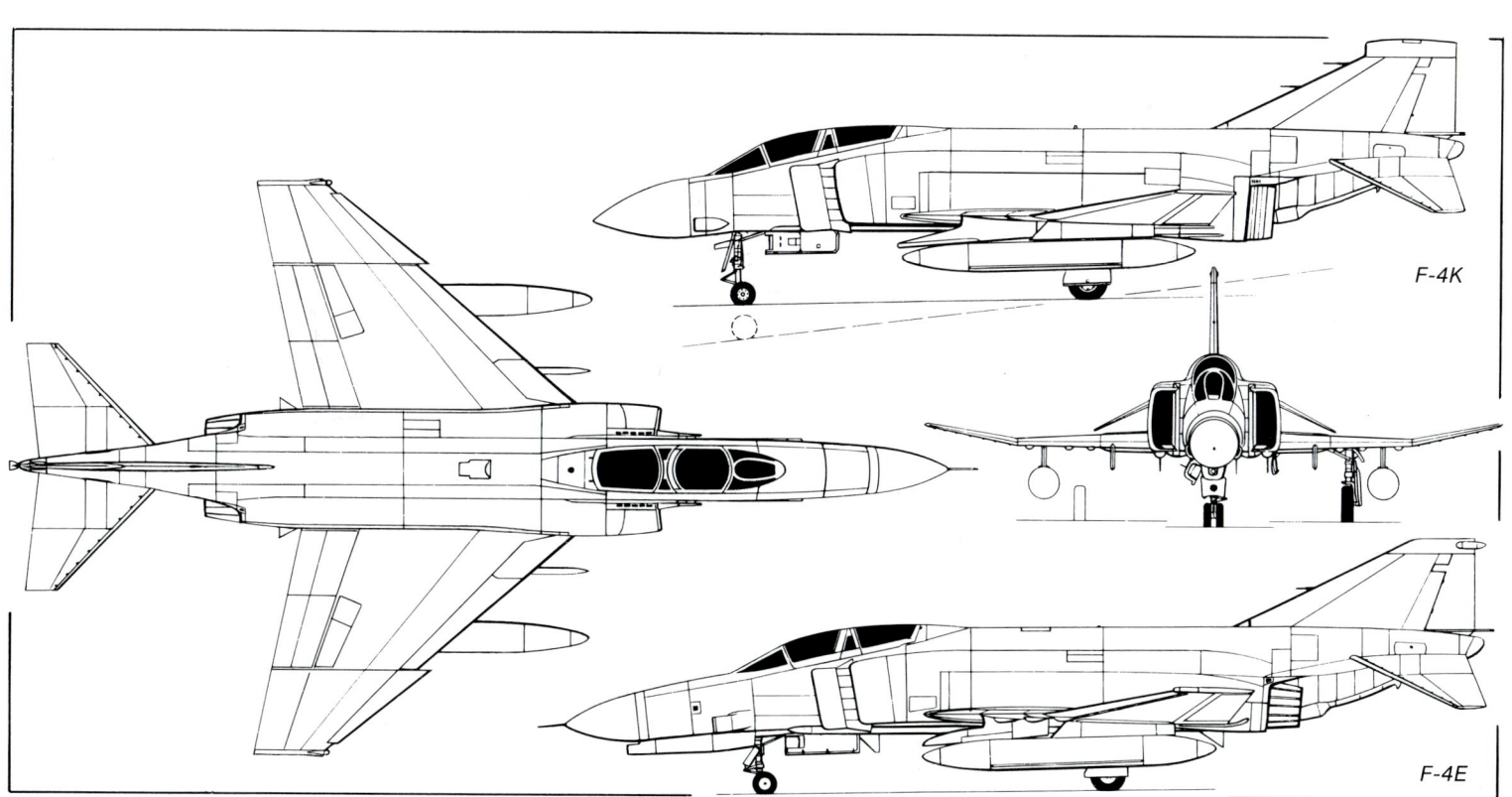

Photographs: pp. 26-27, F-4D; p. 28, F-4 open canopies; p. 29, F-4E; pp. 30-31, F-4 pilot in cockpit; pp. 42-43, F-4Es from F-4 cockpit; pp. 48-49, F-4Es.

F-15

USAF designation: F-15 Eagle
Nickname: Eagle

The F-15 Eagle is an all-weather tactical fighter designed to gain and maintain air superiority in aerial combat. It can outperform and outfight any current or projected enemy aircraft, penetrate enemy defenses, and perform air-to-surface attack with no aircraft modifications.

The F-15's air superiority is achieved through unprecedented maneuverability, acceleration, range, weapons, and avionics. Its weapons and flight control systems are designed so that a single operator can safely and effectively perform air-to-air combat or air-to-surface attack missions.

A head-up display (HUD) projects on the windscreen above the instrument panel at the pilot's eye level all essential flight information. Visible in any light, HUD makes it possible for the pilot to track and destroy enemy aircraft without having to look down at cockpit instruments.

The F-15's versatile pulse-Doppler radar system can "look up" at high-altitude targets and "look down" at tree-top level targets without being confused by ground clutter. The radar feeds target information into a central, on-board, digital computer for effective weapons delivery. An inertial navigation system enables the Eagle to navigate anywhere in the world.

The F-15's tactical electronic warfare system provides both threat warning and automatic countermeasures. An "identification friend or foe" system informs the pilot if an aircraft seen either visually or on radar is friendly. It also informs U.S. or allied ground stations and other suitably equipped aircraft that the F-15 is a friendly aircraft.

Low-drag conformal fuel tanks were specially developed for the F-15. These tanks can be attached to the side of either the left or the right engine air intake trunk. They virtually eliminate in-flight refueling on global missions. The conformal tanks increase aircraft time over a combat area and can also carry cameras or other sensor equipment for reconnaissance missions. The handling characteristics of the F-15 are essentially unchanged with the tanks in place.

The first F-15 Eagle destined for a combat squadron was delivered to the 1st Tactical Fighter Wing at Langley Air Force Base, Virginia, in January 1976. The 36th Tactical Fighter Wing, equipped with F-15s, was deployed to Bitburg Air Base, West Germany, in April 1977.

Primary function: air superiority tactical fighter
Prime contractor: McDonnell Douglas Corp.
Power plant/manufacturer: two Pratt and Whitney F-100-PW-100 turbofan engines with afterburners
Thrust: 25,000 pounds each engine
Dimensions: wingspan 42 feet 9 3/4 inches, length 63 feet 9 inches, height 18 feet 7 1/2 inches
Speed: more than Mach 2.5
Combat ceiling: 65,000 feet
Range: 3,450 miles ferry range with conformal fuel tanks and three external fuel tanks
Crew: one—pilot
Armament: one M-61A1 20mm multibarrel gun mounted internally with 940 rounds of ammunition, four AIM-9L/M Sidewinder and four AIM-7F/M Sparrow missiles, and 15,000 pounds mixed ordnance carried externally
Maximum takeoff weight: 68,000 pounds

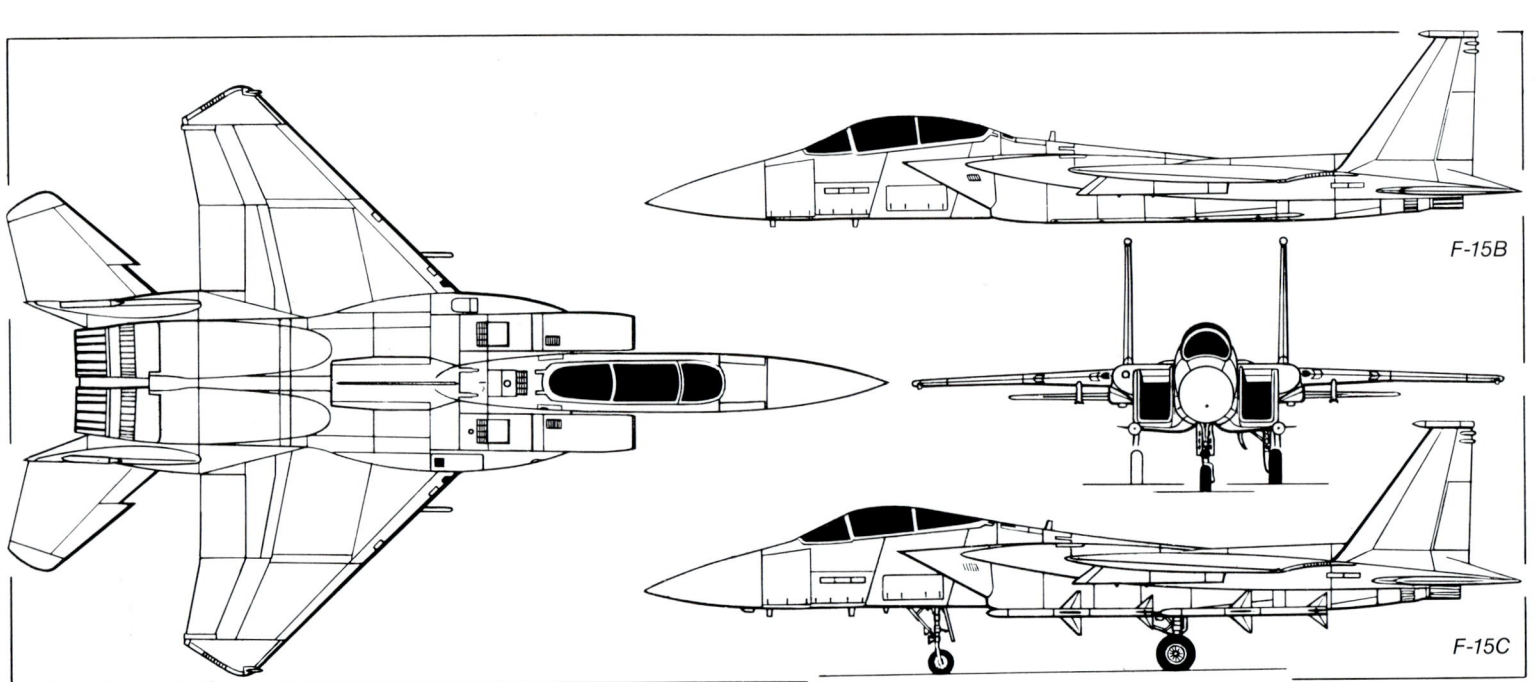

Photographs: pp. 2-3, F-15 cockpit; pp. 6-7, F-15Cs; pp. 12-13, F-15C; p. 14, F-15C; pp. 22-23, F-15D; p. 32, F-15As; p. 33, F-15Cs from F-15D cockpit; pp. 34-35, F-15As; p. 36, all photographs, F-15 pilot in cockpit, takeoff sequence; p. 37, F-15 pilot in cockpit; p. 44, F-15; pp. 52-53, F-15s; pp. 82-83, F-15 cockpit view of KC-135; pp. 98-99, F-15 cockpit view of KC-135 refueling F-15C; p. 128, F-15.

F-16

USAF designation: F-16 Fighting Falcon
Nickname: Electric Jet

The F-16 Fighting Falcon is a compact, multirole fighter aircraft. Highly maneuverable, it is designed for air-to-air combat and air-to-surface attack. For air combat, the F-16's maneuverability and combat radius (distance it can fly to enter air combat, fight, and return) exceed that of all current Warsaw Pact fighter aircraft. In an air-to-surface mission, the F-16 can fly more than 500 miles, fire its weapons with superior accuracy, and return to its starting point.

It has excellent self-defense. Because the F-16 is small and has a smokeless engine, it is difficult to detect, either visually or with radar. Its 360-degree threat warning system reduces the possibility of the pilot being caught by surprise. The aircraft's remarkable maneuverability makes it a difficult target for enemy aircraft and surface-to-air missiles.

The design of the F-16 employs advanced aerospace science and proven systems from other aircraft, including the F-15 and the F-111. The light weight of the fuselage is achieved without reducing its strength. The F-16 can withstand nine Gs with internal fuel tanks filled. The blended-body-and-wing design increases lift at high angles of attack, decreases drag, and adds internal space for fuel and equipment. The wings have leading and trailing edge flaps that automatically change their contour to suit the angle of attack or flight and speed of the aircraft, giving the plane maximum lift-to-drag ratio and minimum buffet through all flight modes.

The cockpit and its bubble canopy give the pilot almost unlimited visibility. Forward and upward vision are unobstructed, and side and rear vision improved. Special adjustments in the pilot's seat and in flight controls enhance the pilot's ability to withstand G forces.

The F-16 is very effective in both air-to-air and air-to-surface missions. The fire control system—including radar, head-up display, and pilot controls—eliminates any need for the pilot to look away from the target. Using the throttle, flight control stick, and ordnance controls the pilot has quick reaction, fingertip control of displays and weapons. The F-16 has all-weather air-to-surface and air-to-air attack capability. It can track low-flying targets under ground clutter conditions. The plane has superior accuracy in weapons delivery under visual conditions and is second only to the F-111 in blind bombing conditions.

The F-16A is the single-seat model of this aircraft. It first flew in December 1976. The first operational F-16A was delivered in January 1979 to the 388th Tactical Fighter Wing at Hill Air Force Base, Utah. The wing trains U.S. and foreign F-16 pilots. The F-16B is the two-seat model. The bubble canopy is extended to accommodate the second cockpit area.

Primary function: fighter, attack
Prime contractor: General Dynamics Corp.
Power plant/manufacturer: one Pratt and Whitney F100-PW-100 turbofan engine with afterburner
Thrust: 25,000 pounds
Dimensions: wingspan 32 feet 8 inches, length 49 feet 5 inches, height 16 feet
Speed: more than Mach 2
Ceiling: above 50,000 feet
Range: more than 2,000 miles ferry range
Crew: F-16A—one—pilot, F-16B—two—pilot, weapons system operator
Armament: one M-61A1 20mm multibarrel cannon with 500 rounds; external stations can carry up to six AIM-9 infrared missiles, conventional air-to-air and air-to-surface munitions, and electronic countermeasure pods
Maximum takeoff weight: 35,400 pounds

Photographs: p. 24, F-16 pilot in cockpit; p. 25, F-16A; pp. 38-39, F-16A Thunderbirds; pp. 40-41, F-16As; pp. 50-51, F-16A.

A-10

USAF designation: A-10 Thunderbolt II
Nickname: Hog, Warthog

The first Air Force aircraft to be designed specifically for close-air support of ground forces, the A-10 Thunderbolt II takes its name from the P-47 Thunderbolt used in World War II for dive bombing and strafing in close-air support. The A-10 is a simple, effective, and survivable twin-engine aircraft that can be used against all ground targets including tanks and other armored vehicles.

Designed to be responsive to the immediate needs of the Army combat commander, the A-10 can loiter for hours in the battle area. It can operate under 1,000-foot ceilings with approximately one-mile visibility. The A-10's short takeoff and landing capability permits operations in and out of locations near the front lines. Many aircraft parts, including engines, main landing gear, and vertical stabilizers, are interchangeable left and right and can be switched in field maintenance conditions. The redundant primary structural parts also enable the aircraft to sustain heavy damage and keep flying. With titanium armor plate protecting the pilot and flight controls, self-sealing fuel cells, and a redundant flight-control hydraulics system backed up by a manual system, the A-10 can survive direct hits from armor-piercing and high-explosive 23mm projectiles.

The single-seat cockpit forward of the wings has a large transparent bubble canopy to provide the pilot all-around vision. It has a bulletproof windscreen, an environmental control system, and a Douglas ejection seat that is operable at speeds from 518 miles per hour down to zero speed at zero altitude.

The weapons delivery system on the A-10 includes a head-up display that gives airspeed, altitude, and dive angle on the windscreen and a Pave Penny laser target-seeking pod under the fuselage. The A-10 also has an armament control panel, a gun camera, and infrared and electronic countermeasures to handle surface-to-air missile threats.

A GAU-8/A Avenger 30mm seven-barrel cannon was designed specifically to give the A-10 tank-killing capability. This gun fires armor-piercing projectiles that are capable of penetrating medium and heavy tanks. The gun also can fire high explosive ammunition for use against trucks and other ground targets. The maneuverability of the A-10 and the cannon's accuracy allow the pilot to bring it into action quickly even under adverse weather and poor visibility conditions. The GAU-8/A cannon fires at either 2,100 or 4,200 rounds per minute.

The first production A-10 flew in October 1975. Delivery of this model began in March 1976 to the 333rd Tactical Fighter Training Wing at Davis-Monthan Air Force Base, Arizona. The first operational wing, the 354th Tactical Fighter Wing at Myrtle Beach Air Force Base, South Carolina, began receiving A-10s in June 1977. The wing became operational in October 1977.

Primary function: close-air support
Prime contractor: Fairchild Republic Company
Power plant/manufacturer: two General Electric TF34-GE-100 turbofan engines
Thrust: 9,065 pounds each engine uninstalled, approximately 8,900 pounds installed
Dimensions: wingspan 57 feet 6 inches, length 53 feet 4 inches, height 14 feet 8 inches
Speed: 443 mph combat speed at 5,000 feet with six Mk-82 laser-guided bombs
Ceiling: can operate under 1,000 feet with one-mile visibility
Range: 250 miles with 9,500 pounds of ordnance and 1.8-hour loiter time
Armament: one GAU-8/A 30mm seven-barrel Gatling gun; up to 16,000 pounds mixed ordnance on eight under-wing and three under-fuselage pylon stations, including 500-pound retarded bombs, 2,000-pound general-purpose bombs, incendiary and Rockeye II cluster bombs, Maverick missiles and laser-guided/electro-optically-guided bombs, infrared countermeasure flares, electronic countermeasure chaff and jammer pods
Crew: one—pilot
Maximum takeoff weight: 46,038 pounds

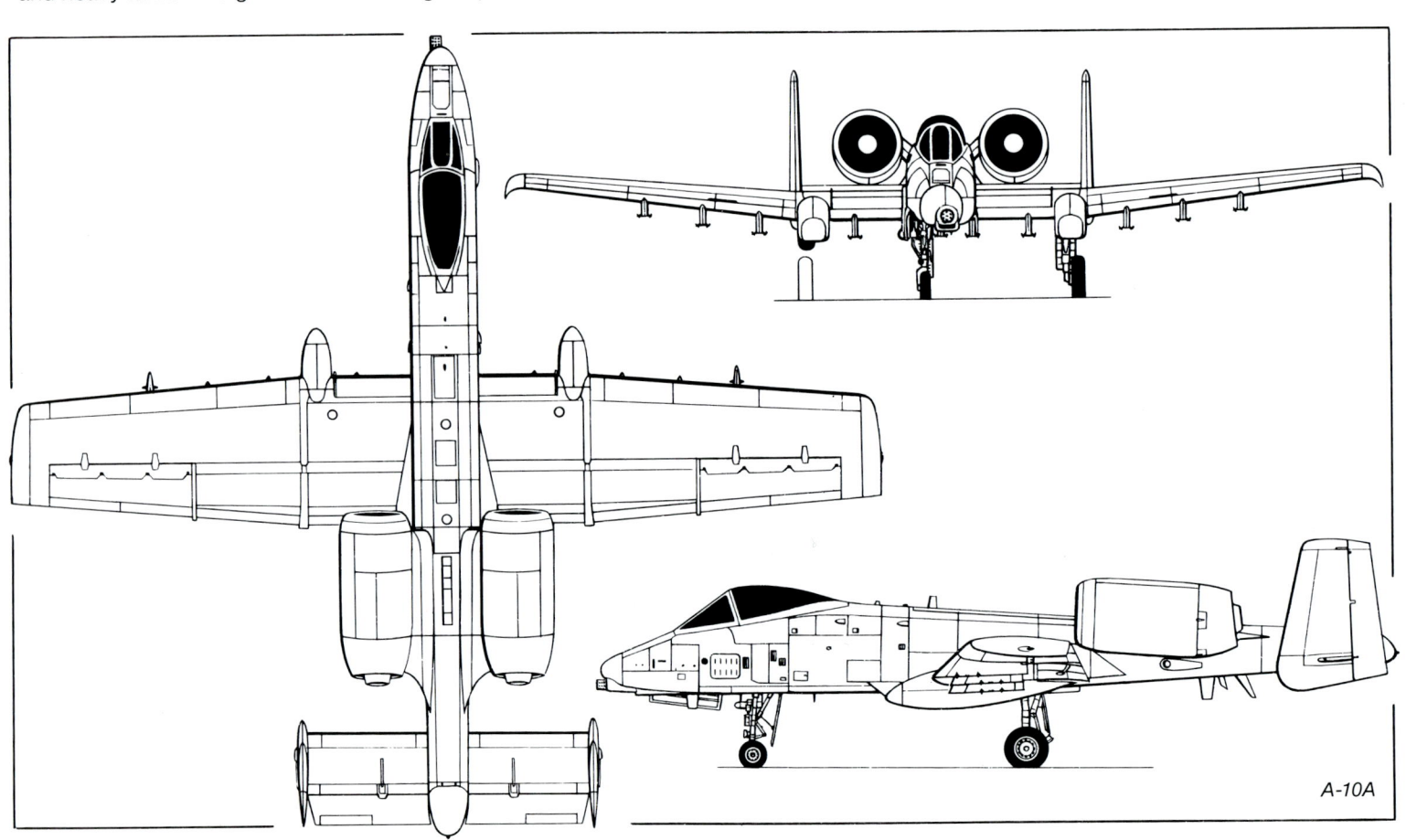

A-10A

Photographs: p. 45, A-10; pp. 46-47, A-10.

B-52

USAF designation: B-52 Stratofortress
Nickname: BUFF, Green Lizard

The B-52 Stratofortress is a long-range, heavy bomber capable of flying at high subsonic speeds at altitudes above 50,000 feet. For more than 20 years, B-52s have been the primary manned strategic bomber force of the United States. The Stratofortress can carry nuclear or conventional ordnance, and in a conventional conflict can perform close-air support, interdiction, and strategic bombing missions. Used to assist the U.S. Navy in anti-ship and anti-submarine operations, the B-52 is highly effective in ocean surveillance. Two B-52s with two hours on station can cover 140,000 square miles of ocean surface.

The B-52A first flew in 1954, and the A model began entering U.S. Air Force service in 1955. A total of 744 B-52s were built, with the last B-52H delivered in 1962. Models A, B, C, E, and F have been phased out of the Air Force inventory.

Delivery of B-52Ds to the Strategic Air Command began in June 1956. All D models were modified to carry a maximum of 108 conventional bombs and were used in the Southeast Asia conflict from 1966 to 1973. In February 1959 deliveries of the B-52G began. The G model is the first missile-carrying bomber. Adaptions included a shorter tail fin, a redesigned wing with integral fuel tanks, and fixed under-wing tanks. The aircraft initially carried two AGM-28 Hound Dog air-to-surface missiles on round-trip missions of more than 10,000 miles.

The first B-52H model was delivered to SAC in May 1961. It has improved defensive armament, including a 20mm Gatling tail gun. Installation of an Air Force satellite communications system on 15 B-52Hs was completed in 1979. The system works in conjunction with orbital stations to give the bombers around-the-world communications capability. With aerial refueling, the B-52's range is limited only by the endurance of its six-man crew.

Modified G and H models can carry up to 20 short-range attack missiles (SRAM)—six under each wing and eight in the bomb bay—as well as four gravity bombs in the bomb bay. All G and H models are equipped with an electro-optical viewing system which uses forward-looking infrared and low-light-level television sensors to improve low-level flight capability.

In the G and H models the gunner's post has been moved from the tail to the forward crew section. The tail guns are controlled by tail-mounted radars. The G and H models have two steerable turrets underneath the nose that contain the electro-optical viewing systems.

B-52G and B-52H models have also been modified to carry the AGM-86B Air-Launched Cruise Missile (ALCM). Each aircraft of the first squadron was modified to carry 12 ALCMs externally. Later modifications incorporated a bomb-bay rotary launcher for eight additional ALCMs, or eight SRAMs, or a combination of the two. In August 1981, the first modified B-52G capable of carrying ALCMs was delivered to Griffiss Air Force Base, New York.

Primary function: strategic heavy bomber
Prime contractor: The Boeing Company
Power plant/manufacturer: eight Pratt and Whitney engines: B-52D—J57-P-29W turbojet, B-52G—J57-P-43W turbojet, B-52H—TF-33-P-3 turbofan
Thrust: each engine: B-52D—up to 12,000 pounds, B-52G—13,750 pounds, B-52H—17,000 pounds
Dimensions: wingspan 185 feet; length B-52D—156 feet 6 inches, B-52G—160 feet 11 inches, B-52H—159 feet 4 inches; height B-52D—48 feet 3 inches, B-52G and H—40 feet 8 inches
Range: unrefueled ferry range B-52D—6,300 miles, B-52G—7,335 miles, B-52H—8,756 miles
Speed: 650 mph maximum at 20,000 feet
Ceiling: above 50,000 feet
Armament: more than 20,000 pounds mixed ordnance, D models modified for 60,000 pounds conventional bombs, B-52G and H—SRAM and ALCM, B-52D and G—four .50 caliber machine guns, B-52H—20mm multibarrel Gatling gun
Crew: six—pilot, copilot, gunner, electronic countermeasures operator, navigator, radar-navigator
Maximum takeoff weight: B-52D—450,000 pounds, B-52G and H—488,000 pounds

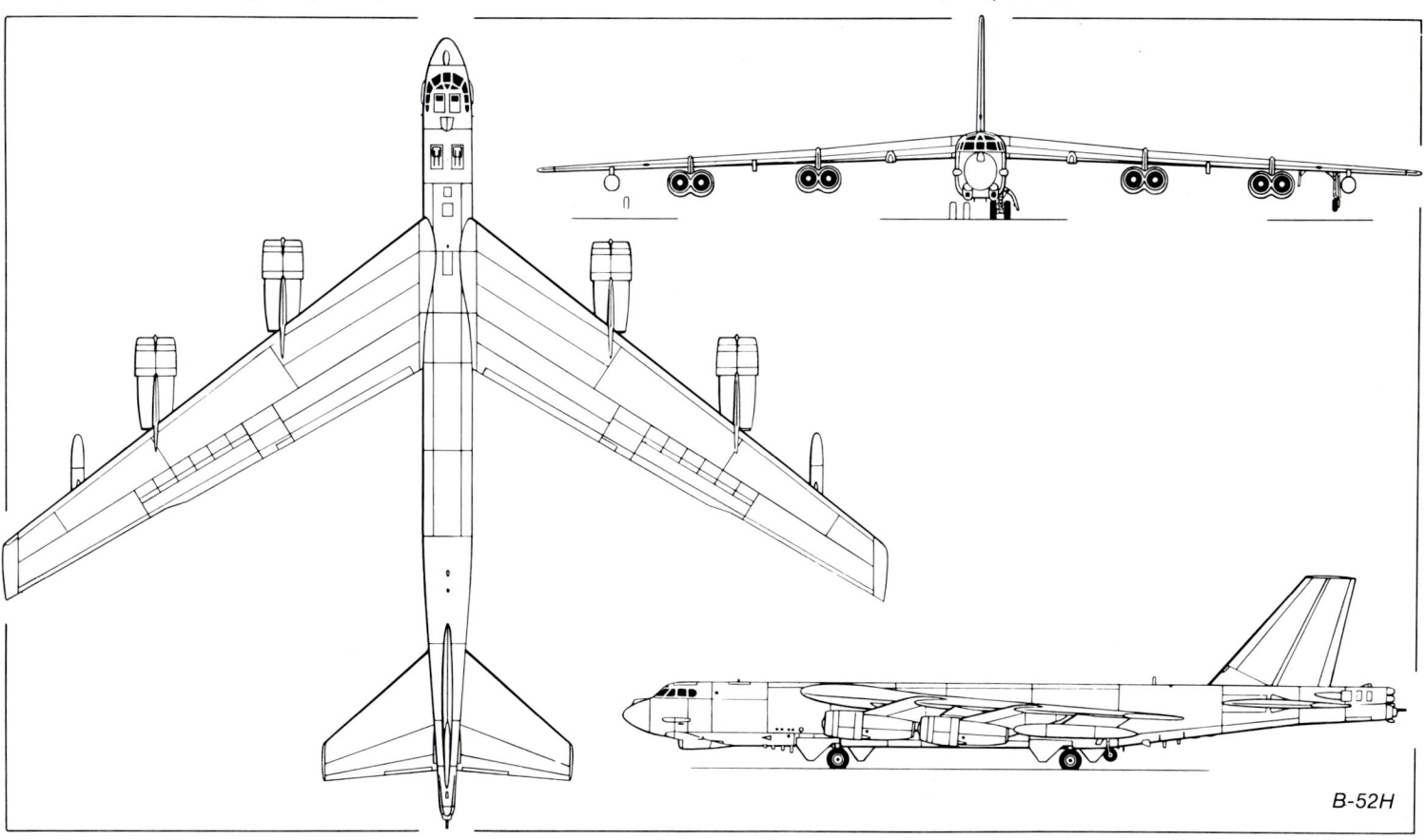

B-52H

Photographs: p. 56, B-52G with ALCM; pp. 58-59, B-52H; pp. 60-61, B-52 pilot and copilot in cockpit; p. 74, B-52; pp. 76-77, B-52H.

FB-111

USAF designation: FB-111A
NICKNAME: Aardvark

The FB-111A is a medium-range, strategic bomber. A variation of the F-111A tactical fighter, it is the first aircraft to combine the maneuverability of a fighter with the payload and range of a bomber. It can carry both nuclear and conventional weapons.

While the FB-111A fuselage is essentially the same as that of the F-111A, the bomber's wings are slightly longer than those of the fighter. The bomber also has strengthened landing gear and increased braking capacity.

Variable-sweep wings are an important feature of the aircraft. By moving the wings to different positions, a pilot can fly the FB-111 from slow approach speeds to supersonic speed at sea level, and to more than twice the speed of sound above 60,000 feet. The pilot changes the wings' angle in flight or on the ground by moving a lever on the left panel of his cockpit. The lever controls hydraulic actuators that push the wings back by extending large internal screws or contracting the screws to pull the wings forward. Wing angles from 16 degrees (full forward) to 72.5 degrees (full rear sweep) are possible. When wings are fully swept in what is called the "delta" position, the tips rest close to the horizontal stabilizers. Wings in full forward position give maximum surface area and lift for short takeoff and landing.

The crew of two sit side-by-side in an air-conditioned, pressurized cockpit module. The module serves as an emergency escape vehicle and survival shelter on land or water. If ejection is necessary, both crew members remain in the cockpit. An explosive cutting cord separates the module from the fuselage and a rocket motor propels it away from the aircraft. The module descends by parachute. Airbags cushion impact and keep the aircraft afloat if it lands in water. The module can be released at any speed and altitude—even under water.

External ordnance and fuel tanks can be carried on six pylons under the wings. On each side, the two pylons nearest the fuselage pivot as the wings sweep back, keeping the ordnance parallel to the fuselage. The outer attachment on each wing, used only in subsonic flight, does not pivot and is jettisoned before the wings can be swept past 26 degrees.

A radar bombing system is used for precise weapons delivery during the day, at night, or in bad weather. The automatic terrain-following radar system flies the FB-111 at selectable heights following the earth's contours. TFR guides the aircraft into valleys and over mountains, day or night, regardless of weather conditions. Should any of the radar system's circuits fail, the aircraft automatically climbs to a safe altitude.

The first production FB-111A was delivered in October 1969 to the 340th Bombardment Group at Carswell Air Force Base, Texas.

Primary function: medium-range strategic bomber
Prime contractor: General Dynamics Corp.
Power plant/manufacturer: two Pratt and Whitney TF30-P-7 turbofan engines with variable afterburners
Thrust: 20,350 pounds each engine
Dimensions: wingspan—spread 70 feet, fully swept 33 feet 11 inches, length 73 feet 6 inches, height 17 feet 1 inch
Speed: Mach 2.5 at 36,000 feet
Ceiling: above 60,000 feet
Range: 4,100 miles with external fuel tanks
Ordnance: up to four AGM-69A SRAM air-to-surface missiles on external pylons and two in weapons bay, or six nuclear bombs, or combinations of these weapons; provision for up to 31,500 pounds of conventional bombs
Crew: two—pilot and navigator-bombardier
Maximum takeoff weight: about 100,000 pounds

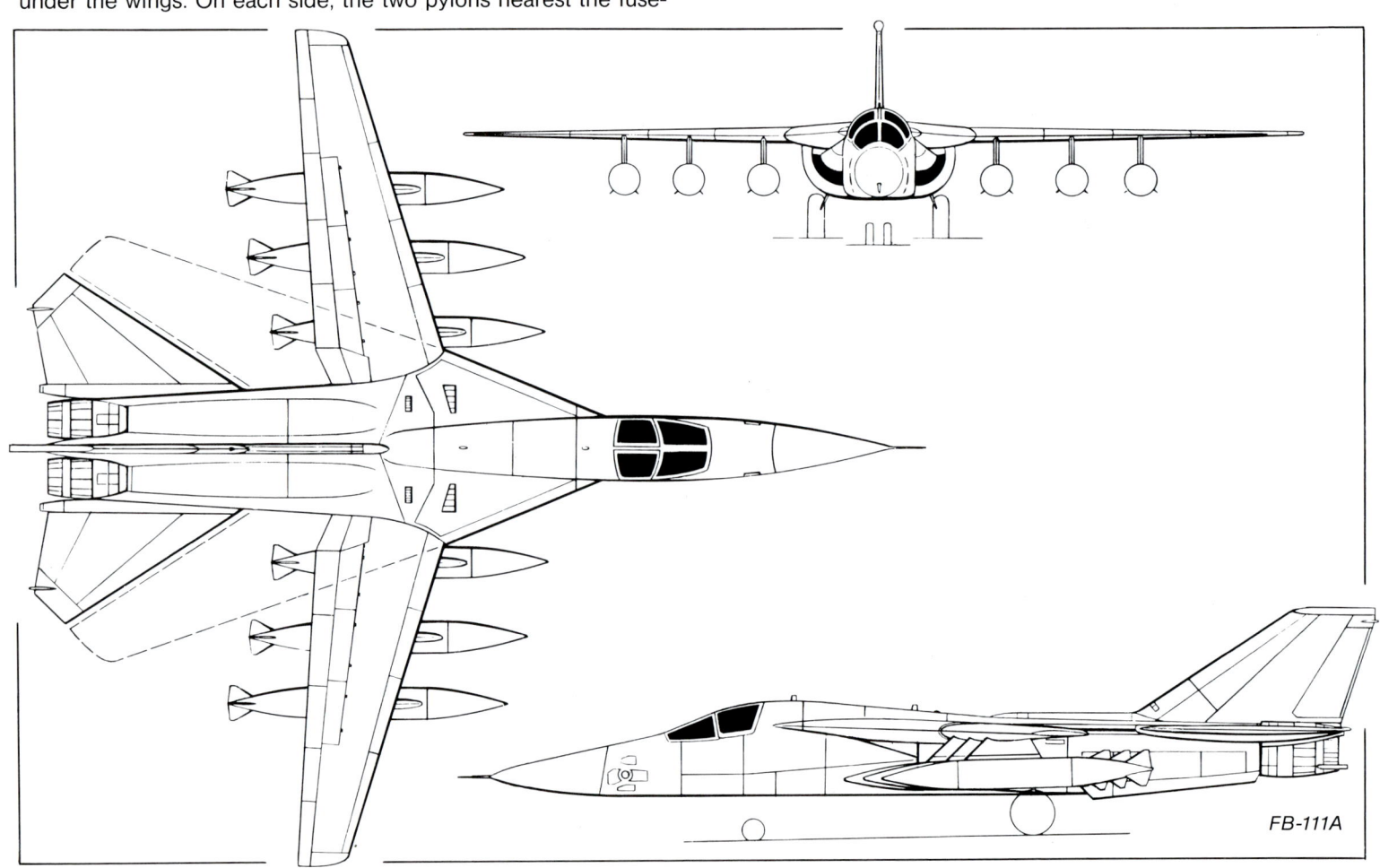

Photographs: pp. 10-11, FB-111A; p. 21, FB-111A being refueled by KC-135; p. 63, FB-111A; pp. 64-65, FB-111As; pp. 66-67, FB-111As; p. 68, FB-111A cockpit; p. 72, FB-111A; p. 92, FB-111A viewed from KC-135 boom pod.

B-1

USAF designation: B-1B
Nickname: none

The B-1B is being developed to modernize the strategic bomber fleet. Its advanced avionics equipment and reduced radar cross section will aid in penetration of enemy defenses. The B-1B will carry heavy weapons payloads.

Studies for the B-1 were initiated in 1965. Characteristics planned for the advanced bomber were established following detailed studies of strategic concepts and numerous point designs. The B-1B is a derivative aircraft which has been developed in response to strategic needs.

The United States' strategic deterrent depends heavily on the Strategic Air Command bomber force. This manned strategic bomber force can respond to changing combat situations and provides several options to the National Command Authority. The core of this force is the B-52, which has been modernized, but whose fundamental technology was developed in the 1950s.

The B-1B takes advantage of the many advances made in airframe, engine, and avionics during the past 20 years. It will become a viable weapon in the mixed-force concept of manned bombers, land-launched, and sea-launched missiles.

The aircraft is designed to be compatible with KC-135 and KC-10 tankers, but is capable of intercontinental missions without aerial refueling. It has quick takeoff capability and improved hardness to nuclear weapons effects, which will improve the bomber force's ability to survive a surprise enemy submarine-launched missile attack.

The B-1B can carry practically any type ordnance now in the Air Force inventory, plus advanced weapons which are being studied or developed. Weapons-carrying capability includes gravity, Short Range Attack Missile (SRAM), and Air-Launched Cruise Missile (ALCM).

Primary function: strategic heavy bomber
Prime contractor: Rockwell International Corp.
Power plant/manufacturer: four General Electric F101-GE-102 turbofan engines with afterburners
Thrust: approximately 30,000 pounds each engine
Dimensions: wingspan—spread 137 feet, fully swept 78 feet, length 147 feet, height 34 feet
Speed: low supersonic; high subsonic for low-altitude penetration
Ceiling: CLASSIFIED
Range: intercontinental unrefueled
Ordnance: approximately twice payload of B-52; SRAM, nuclear gravity, ALCM, conventional
Crew: four—pilot, copilot, offensive system operator, defensive system operator
Maximum takeoff weight: 477,000 pounds

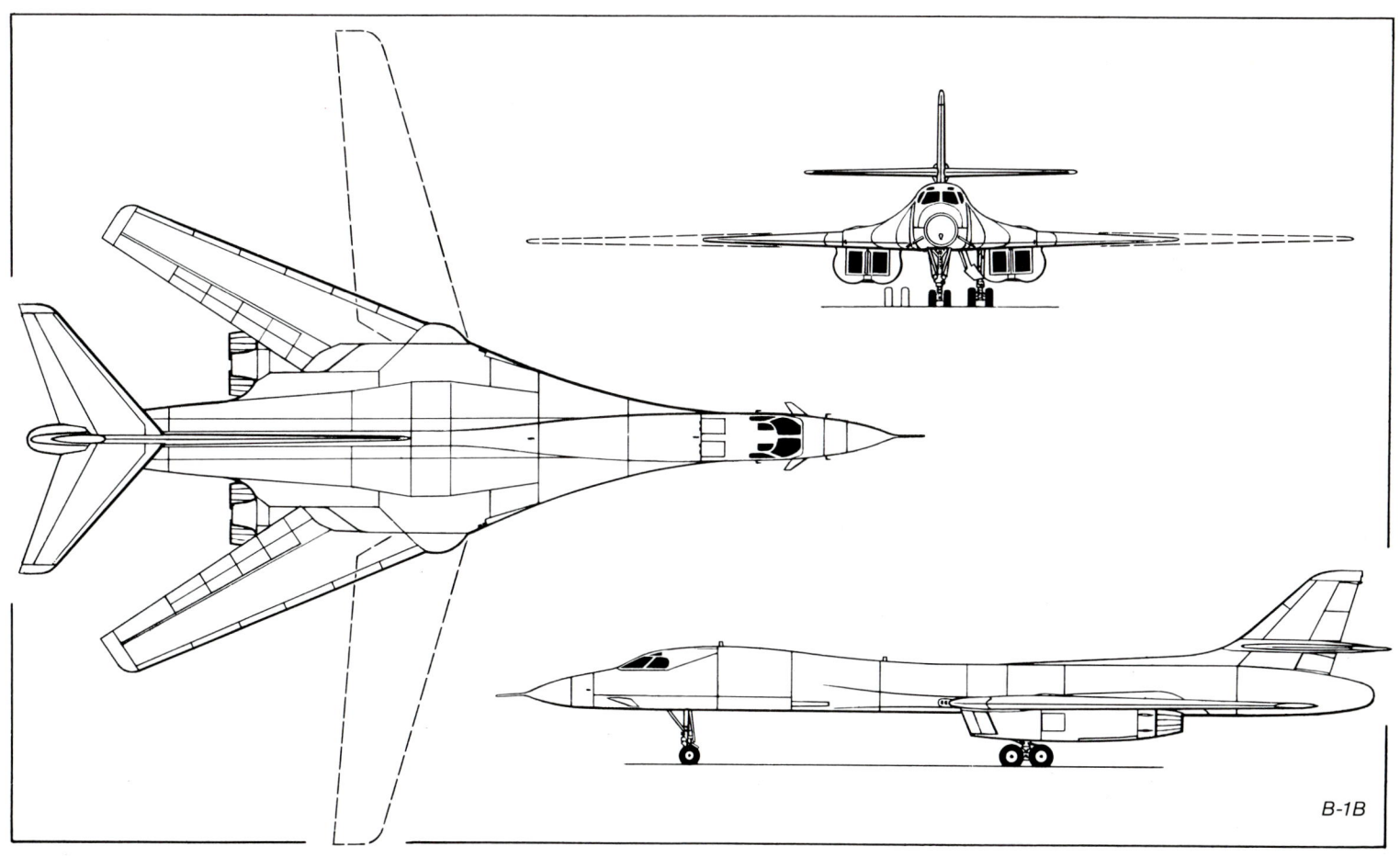

B-1B

Photographs: pp. 54-55, B-1B; p. 57, B-1B; p. 62, B-1B engine detail; p. 69, B-1B; pp. 70-71, B-1B; p. 73, B-1B; p. 75, B-1B.

C-141

USAF designation: C-141 Starlifter
Nickname: Starlifter

The C-141 provides long-range transport at jet speeds and has been the workhorse of military airlift forces since it entered the Air Force inventory in 1965. Compared with earlier transports, the C-141's high cruise speed, transoceanic range, greater cargo capacity, short takeoff and landing capability, and mechanized on- and off-loading have reduced cost and delivery time for airlift missions. The C-141 can carry up to 70,000 pounds of cargo non-stop for 3,500 miles and regularly flies non-stop from Dover Air Force Base, Delaware, to West Germany. With smaller loads, the C-141 can fly non-stop from San Francisco to Tokyo.

The C-141 is the first aircraft designed to be compatible with the 463L Materiel Handling System, which permits off-loading 68,000 pounds of cargo, refueling, and reloading a full cargo in less than one hour's time. Its cargo compartment can be easily modified to perform approximately 30 different missions. About 150 troops or 123 fully-equipped paratroops can sit in rear-facing airline seats or canvas side-facing seats. Rollers in the aircraft floor allow quick and easy cargo pallet loading. When palletized cargo is not being carried, the rollers can be turned over, providing a flat surface for loading vehicles. In its aeromedical evacuation role, the C-141 can carry about 80 litter patients or 120 ambulatory patients.

The first C-141A was delivered to Tinker Air Force Base, Oklahoma, in October 1964, and squadron operations began in April 1965. Almost daily, Starlifters flew to Southeast Asia carrying troops, equipment, and supplies and bringing back the sick and wounded to U.S. hospitals.

A total of 284 C-141s were built. It is the first jet transport from which U.S. Army paratroopers have jumped and the first to land in the Antarctic. A C-141 established a world record for heavy cargo drops—70,195 pounds. Several C-141s have been modified to carry the Minuteman Intercontinental Ballistic Missile in its special container—a total weight of 86,207 pounds. Some C-141s have been equipped with Intraformation Positioning Sets that enable a flight of two to 36 aircraft to maintain formation regardless of visibility. The first production C-141B, with a lengthened fuselage increasing cargo capacity by 30 percent and in-flight refueling capability, was delivered to the Air Force in December 1979.

Primary function: long-range troop and cargo airlift
Prime contractor: Lockheed-Georgia Company
Power plant/manufacturer: four Pratt and Whitney TF33-P-7 turbofan engines
Thrust: 21,000 pounds each engine
Dimensions: wingspan 159 feet 11 inches, length 145 feet, height 39 feet 3 inches
Speed: 490 mph cruising speed at 35,000 feet
Range: 3,500 miles with 70,000 pounds cargo
Crew: five—pilot, copilot, load master, two flight engineers
Maximum takeoff weight: 323,000 pounds

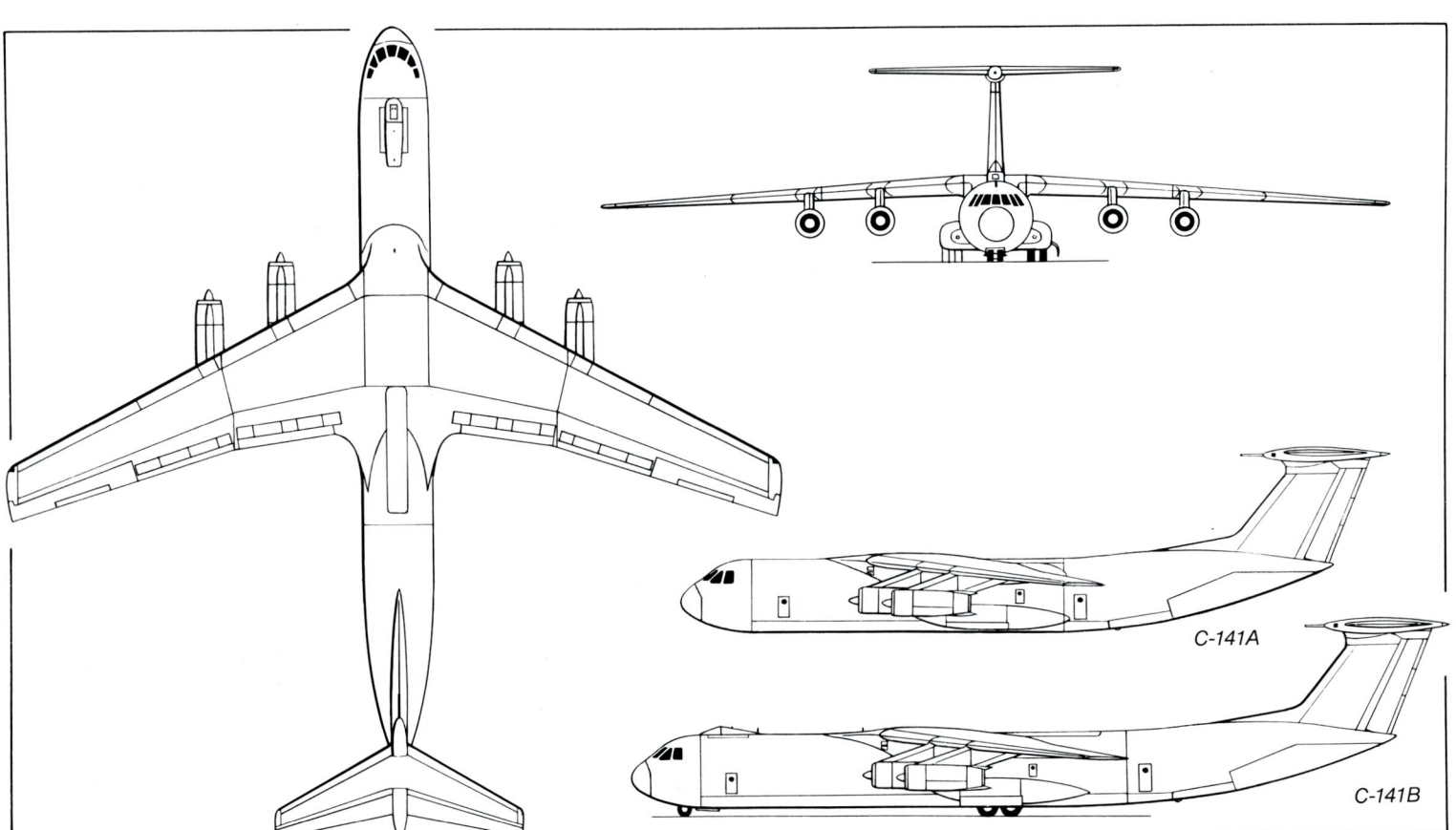

Photographs: p. 80, C-141 engineer at console; pp. 84-85, C-141s (foreground); pp. 86-87, C-141s dropping paratroops.

C-5

USAF designation: C-5 Galaxy
Nickname: Galaxy, Fat Albert, FRED

The C-5 Galaxy is a heavy-cargo transport designed to provide massive strategic airlift for deployment and supply of combat and support forces. It can carry unusually large and heavy cargo at intercontinental ranges and jet speeds, can take off and land in relatively short distances, and can taxi on substandard surfaces during emergency operations.

The C-5, transporting bulky, heavy cargo, and the C-141, carrying personnel and less bulky, lighter cargo, are strategic airlift partners. On short notice they can carry fully equipped, combat-ready divisions to any area in the world and provide the full field support required to maintain the fighting force. Except in emergencies or unusual circumstances, the C-5 does not carry troops in its lower-deck cargo compartment. The rear compartment of the upper deck has 73 seats available for operators of equipment being airlifted and other personnel. The forward upper deck has accommodations for a crew of seven, a relief crew of seven, and eight mail or message couriers. This flight deck has work stations for the pilot, copilot, navigator, flight engineer, and three observers or instructors.

The Galaxy can be loaded and off-loaded simultaneously. A visor nose and a rear door, each with full-width ramps, open to expose the full height and width of the cargo compartment, permitting drive-through loading and unloading of wheeled and tracked vehicles, and faster and easier loading of bulky equipment. A "kneeling" landing gear system lowers the aircraft's cargo floor to truckbed height, and the entire cargo floor is equipped with a roller system for rapid handling of palletized equipment.

The C-5 can take off fully loaded within 12,200 feet and land within 4,900 feet. Its massive weight is distributed on high-flotation landing gear with 28 wheels. This system can raise each set of wheels individually for tire change or brake maintenance and can deflate the tires for landing on unimproved surfaces. The Galaxy has 12 integral-wing fuel tanks with a capacity of 49,000 gallons—enough to fill more than six railroad tank cars. Sophisticated communications equipment and a triple inertial navigation system enable the C-5 to operate without the aid of ground-based navigational equipment.

The first operational Galaxys were delivered to the 437th Military Airlift Wing, Charleston Air Force Base, South Carolina, in June 1970, followed by delivery to the 60th Military Airlift Wing at Travis Air Force Base, California, in October 1970, and to Dover Air Force Base, Delaware, in April 1971.

Primary function: long-range, heavy logistics transport
Prime contractor: Lockheed-Georgia Company
Power plant/manufacturer: four General Electric TF39-GE-1 turbofan engines
Thrust: 40,100 pounds each engine
Dimensions: wingspan 222 feet 9 inches, length 247 feet 10 inches, height 65 feet 1 inch, cargo compartment—height 13 feet 6 inches, width 19 feet
Speed: more than 495 mph at 25,000 feet with takeoff weight 769,000 pounds
Ceiling: 34,000 feet at 615,000 pounds weight
Range: 5,930 miles with 112,600 pounds cargo at 507 mph
Load: current C-5—204,904 pounds maximum wartime load, with wing modifications—242,500 pounds maximum wartime load
Crew: seven to eight—pilot, copilot, flight engineers, navigator, loadmasters
Maximum takeoff weight: 769,000 pounds

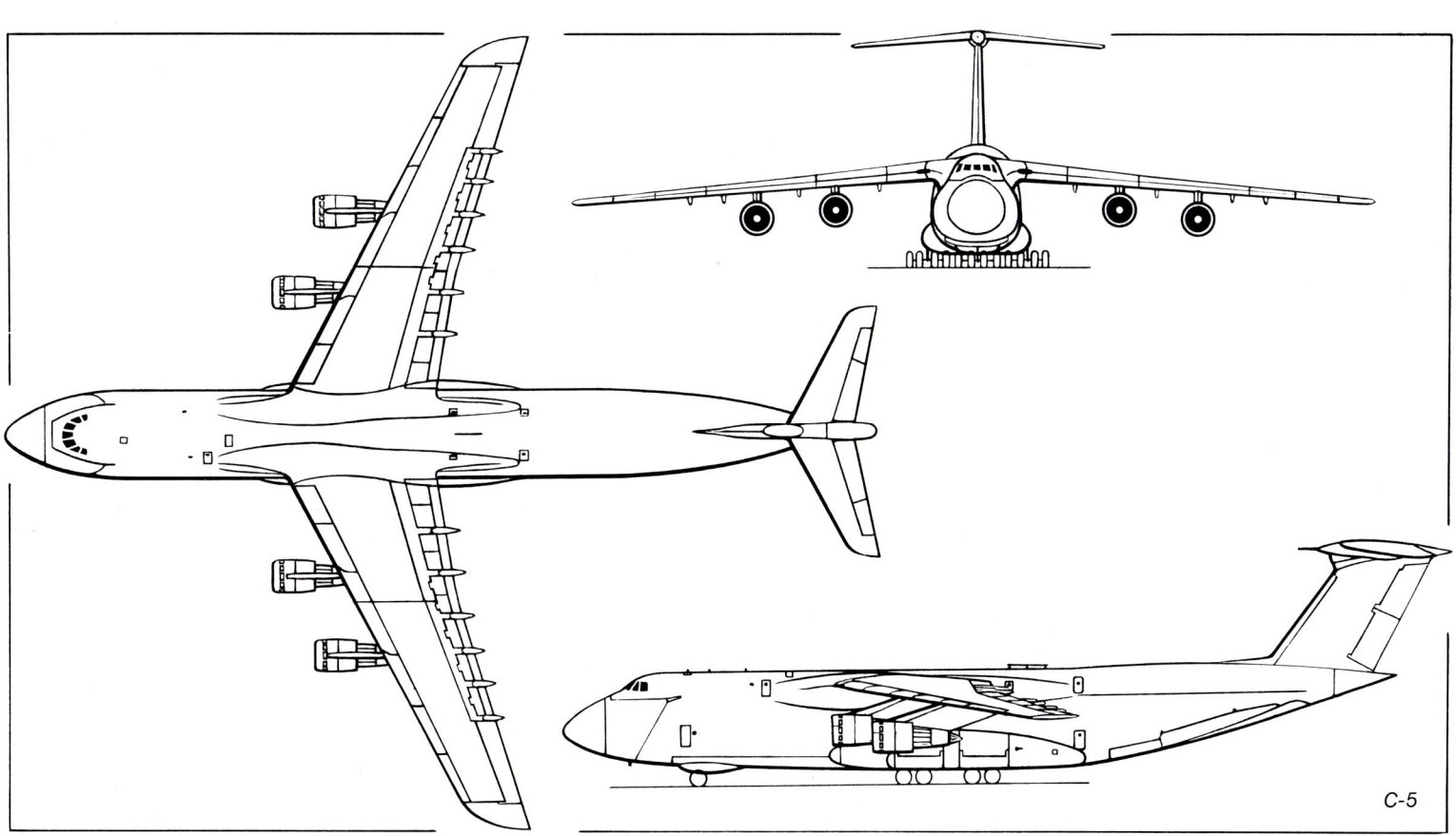

Photographs: pp. 78-79, C-5; p. 81, C-5; pp. 84-85, C-5 (background); p. 88, C-5; pp. 88-89, C-5; pp. 90-91, C-5s; p. 100 inset, C-5; pp. 100-101, C-5.

AC-130

USAF designation: AC-130H Hercules
Nickname: Specter, Hercules, Herky Bird

The AC-130A and H Hercules aircraft are gunship models of the C-130A and H. They are specially equipped to perform close-air support, armed reconnaissance, and air interdiction missions. Beginning in 1968 the gunships were used in the Southeast Asia conflict, where they were given the nickname "Specter."

These heavily-armed aircraft have side-firing weapons linked by on-board computer to a highly sophisticated sensor system. Forward-looking infrared target acquisition equipment, low-light-level TV camera, and laser target designators give the AC-130 night operation capability. The gunships also have a two-kilowatt searchlight that can be operated as an infrared system.

The AC-130 has been employed extensively in peacetime night search and rescue missions using its infrared and low-light-level TV detection systems. When a commercial airliner crashed in the Everglades near Miami in 1973, a gunship orbited the area for hours, using its two-kilowatt searchlight to locate and direct rescue workers to victims in the scattered wreckage. Since then, the aircraft has been used in search and rescue operations in other parts of the nation.

All the AC-130As were transferred from the active force to the Air Force Reserve in 1975. They are operated by the 919th Special Operations Group at Duke Field in Florida which is the Reserve's only special operations group. These aircraft are armed with two 7.62mm Miniguns, two 20mm Vulcan cannons, and two 40mm Bofors cannon. The guns on the A model have a total firepower capability of over 17,000 rounds per minute.

The active Air Force has ten AC-130Hs assigned to the 16th Special Operations Squadron of the 1st Special Operations Wing at Hurlburt Field, Florida. These aircraft have the same armament as the A models, except a 105mm howitzer replaces one of the 40mm cannon. The H model also has in-flight refueling capability.

Primary function: armed reconnaissance, close-air support, air interdiction
Prime contractor: Lockheed Aircraft Corp.
Power plant/manufacturer: four Allison turboprop engines: AC-130A—T56-A-9C, AC-130H—T56-A-15
Horsepower: each engine: AC-130A—3,750 hp, AC-130H—4,508 hp
Dimensions: wingspan 132 feet 7 inches, length 97 feet 9 inches, height 38 feet 3 inches
Speed: 336 mph at maximum takeoff weight
Ceiling: above 25,000 feet
Range: AC-130A—1,950 miles, AC-130H—2,450 miles
Armament: AC-130A—two 7.62mm Miniguns, two 20mm Vulcan cannon, two 40mm Bofors cannon; AC-130H has one 40mm cannon replaced by a 105mm howitzer
Crew: 14—five officers and nine enlisted
Maximum takeoff weight: AC-130A—124,000 pounds, AC-130H—155,000 pounds

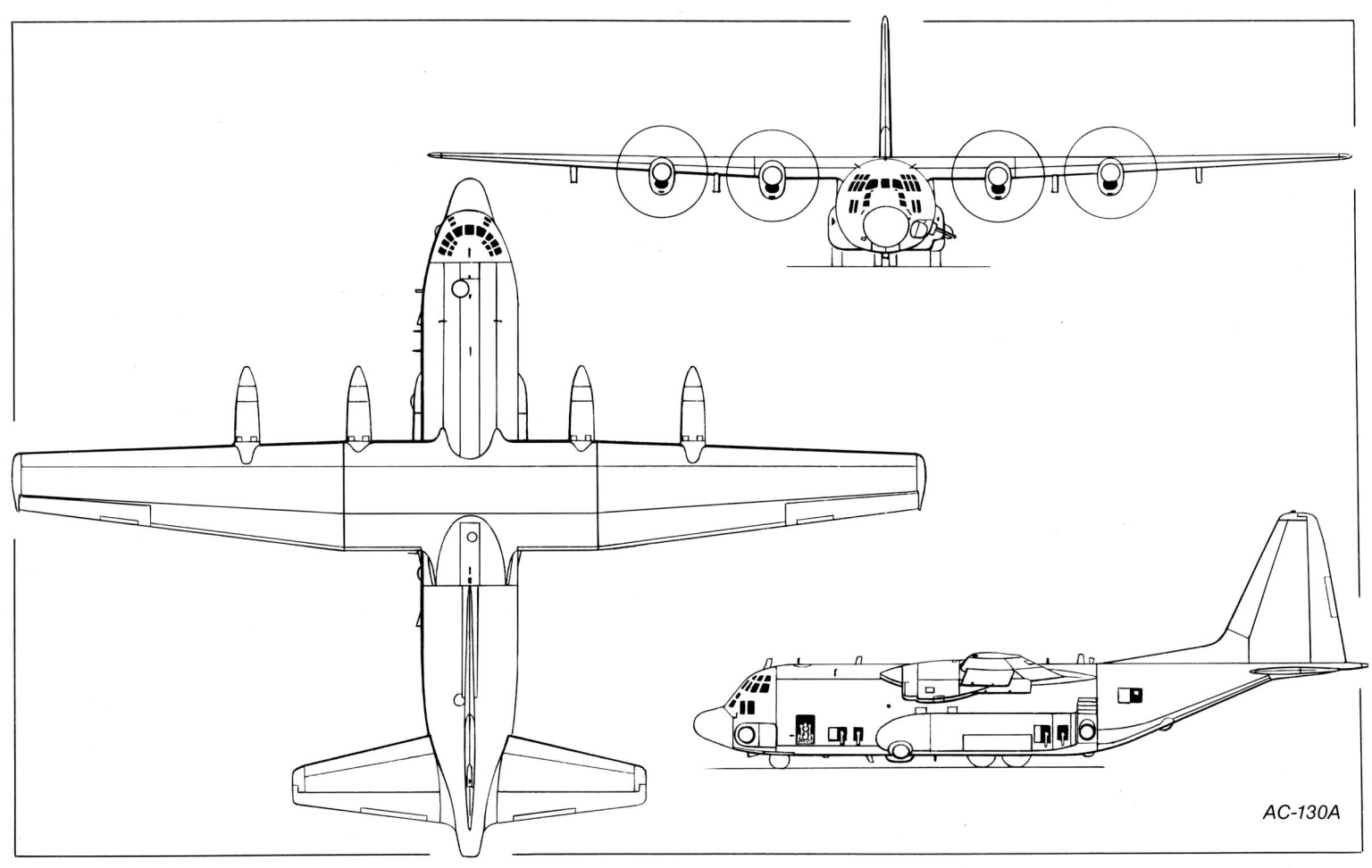

AC-130A

Photographs: p. 4, C-130E; p. 96, AC-130H; p. 97, AC-130H.

KC-135

USAF designation: KC-135 Stratotanker
Nickname: Stratotanker

KC-135 Stratotankers have been used by the Air Force for more than 20 years. A military version of the Boeing 707 passenger plane, the KC-135 replaced the KC-97, a propeller-driven tanker which could not meet the performance requirements of the increasing number of jet bombers and fighters it supported. Jets had to drop from cruising altitudes and slow to near-stall speeds to hook up with the KC-97. The KC-135's work altitude of 40,000 feet and cruising speed of 530 mph more nearly match the performance of the other jet aircraft it refuels.

Since the KC-135's primary strategic job is refueling long-range bombers, the active-duty tanker fleet is owned and managed by the Strategic Air Command. SAC has approximately 640 KC-135s that perform a variety of training and aircraft movement missions, both within the continental U.S. and overseas. Another 128, flown by Guard and Reserve forces, support SAC's mission.

All internal fuel, except 1,200 gallons, can be pumped through the flying boom, the KC-135's primary method of transferring fuel. An operator stationed in the rear of the plane is responsible for controlling the boom. A cargo deck above the refueling gear can carry both passengers and cargo. Depending on the amount of fuel in the center wing tank, fuselage loads of up to 83,000 pounds can be accommodated.

KC-135s made the air war in Southeast Asia different from all previous aerial conflicts. Combat bomber and fighter operations were no longer limited by on-board fuel. Pilots were able to spend more time over target areas, and distant bombing targets were brought within reach. Tanker response to emergency situations also accounted for numerous documented aircraft "saves."

A portion of the Stratotanker force is maintained on 24-hour ground alert in support of the Single Integrated Operational Plan (SIOP)—the nation's nuclear weapons contingency plan. Many KC-135s have been altered to do jobs ranging from flying command post missions to reconnaissance. KC-135Rs and Ts are used for special reconnaissance. Other models include the KC-135Q, which refuels SR-71s, and the JKC- and NKC-135A, which are flown by the Air Force Systems Command in test programs.

The initial production Stratotanker was delivered to Castle Air Force Base, California, in June 1957.

Primary function: aerial refueling
Prime contractor: The Boeing Company
Power plant/manufacturer: four Pratt and Whitney J-57-P-59W turbojet engines
Thrust: 13,750 pounds each engine
Dimensions: wingspan 130 feet 10 inches, length 136 feet 3 inches, height 38 feet 4 inches
Speed: 530 mph at 30,000 feet
Ceiling: 50,000 feet
Range: 1,150 miles with 120,000 pounds of transfer fuel; ferry mission 9,200 miles
Crew: four—pilot, copilot, navigator, and boom operator
Maximum takeoff weight: 297,000 pounds

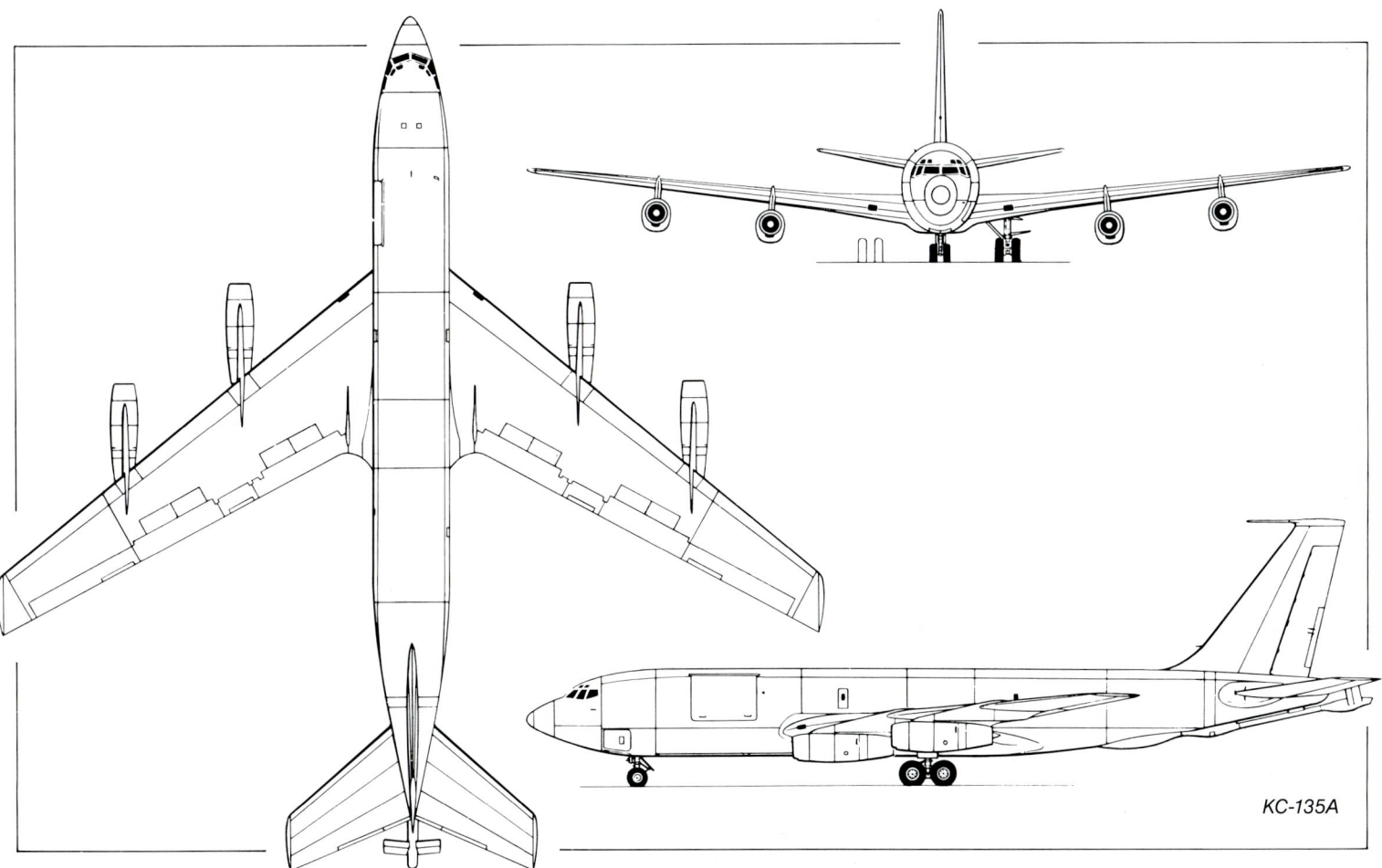

KC-135A

Photographs: p. 21, KC-135 refueling FB-111A; pp. 82-83, KC-135 from F-15 cockpit; p. 92, KC-135 boom pod view of FB-111A; p. 93, KC-135; pp. 98-99, F-15 cockpit view of KC-135 refueling F-15C; pp. 122-123, KC-135 refueling E-3A.

KC-10

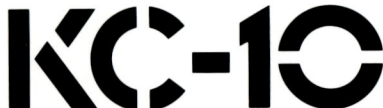

USAF designation: KC-10A Extender
Nickname: none

The KC-10A Extender is an advanced tanker-cargo aircraft providing U.S. forces with increased global mobility. Operated by the Strategic Air Command, the KC-10 provides aerial refueling for many types of aircraft, including fighters, bombers, and cargo aircraft deploying overseas.

While performing its primary mission of aerial refueling, the KC-10A can transport up to 75 people and approximately 170,000 pounds of cargo. In this dual role, it has a range of about 4,400 miles. On a non-refueling mission, the KC-10 has an unrefueled range of more than 11,500 miles and is itself refuelable. By employing a traditional boom or an extended hose system the KC-10 can refuel a wide variety of U.S. military and allied aircraft. The KC-10 is equipped with special lighting to aid night-time refueling operations.

The KC-10A boom operator carries out refueling operations using a digital, "fly-by-wire" control system similar to the controls in the F-16 fighter. In the KC-10, the boom operator sits upright in the rear of the aircraft and is able to observe the receiver through a wide viewing window. During boom refueling operations, fuel is transferred to receiver aircraft at a rate of 1,500 gallons per minute. Drogue refueling off-load rate is 600 gallons per minute.

The sophisticated avionics of the aircraft are designed to improve crew efficiency and reduce crew workload. On certain missions, additional seats and bunks can be arranged in several different configurations to accommodate additional crew members.

The KC-10A uses the worldwide support system of its civilian counterpart, the McDonnell Douglas DC-10 cargo plane. Most major maintenance can be taken care of at commercial facilities, leaving only routine and flight line maintenance to be done by Air Force personnel. This procedure makes it easier and less expensive to repair the KC-10 overseas.

KC-10A squadrons are located at Barksdale Air Force Base, Louisiana, and March Air Force Base, California, and are flown by crews assigned to the 2nd Bombardment Wing and the 22nd Air Refueling Wing. Aircrews are also provided by Air Force Reserve associated units at Barksdale and March.

Primary function: aerial tanker and transport
Prime contractor: Douglas Aircraft Company, McDonnell Douglas Corporation
Power plant/manufacturer: three General Electric CF6-50C2 turbofan engines
Thrust: 52,500 pounds each engine
Dimensions: wingspan 165 feet 3 inches, length 181 feet 6 inches, height 57 feet 7 inches, cargo space—12,000 cubic feet
Speed: more than 500 mph
Ceiling: 42,000 feet
Range: unrefueled—11,500 miles
Crew: four—pilot, copilot, flight engineer, and boom operator
Maximum load: 350,000 pounds
Maximum takeoff weight: 590,000 pounds

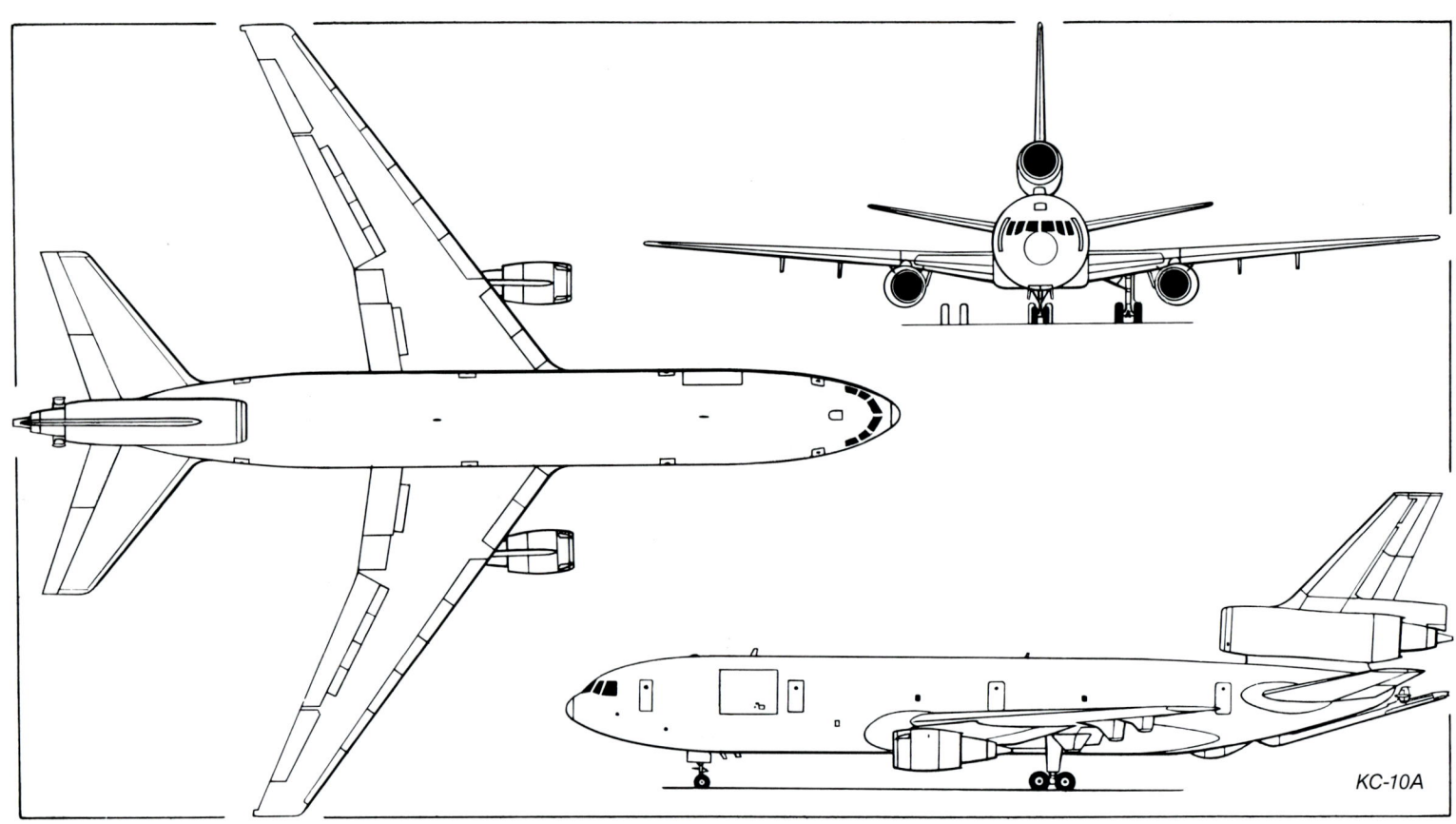

Photographs: pp. 94-95, KC-10.

U-2

USAF designation: U-2
Nickname: none

The U-2 is a single-engine, high-altitude, reconnaissance aircraft. Long, wide, straight wings give it glider-like characteristics and increase its load capacity to accommodate data collection instruments. It can operate above 70,000 feet and "loiter" in an area for hours at a time.

The U-2 made its first flight in August 1955. Several U-2s remain in service with the U.S. Air Force's 9th Strategic Reconnaissance Wing at Beale Air Force Base, California, and the National Aeronautics and Space Administration. They are used for high-altitude reconnaissance and air sampling flights.

Since 1957, a series of U-2 flights has been conducted to sample radioactive debris in the stratosphere. Data collected from these worldwide missions contribute significantly to the understanding of the environment and provide valuable scientific data. On October 14, 1962, the U-2 obtained the first photographs of the Soviet military buildup and offensive-missile installations in Cuba.

Air Force U-2s have also provided important nonmilitary mission support. Numerous missions have been flown in support of the Department of Agriculture land management and crop estimate programs. The U-2 has been used to make photographs for the Army Corps of Engineers for flood control studies and for state governments to determine damage from floods, hurricanes, and tornadoes. Other U-2 projects include obtaining data for the geothermal energy program and participation in search missions for missing boats and aircraft.

In October 1976, U-2 missions helped the U.S. Coast Guard locate a sailor who had been adrift in the Pacific Ocean for 28 days. Analysis of film from U-2 missions in the area enabled the Coast Guard to narrow their search to a 600-square-mile area, resulting in the rescue of the survivor from a life raft about 780 miles west of San Francisco.

Primary function: high-altitude reconnaissance and air sampling
Prime contractor: Lockheed Aircraft Corp.
Power plant/manufacturer: one Pratt and Whitney J75-P-13 turbojet engine
Thrust: 17,000 pounds
Dimensions: wingspan 103 feet, length 63 feet, height 16 feet
Speed: 430 mph
Range: more than 3,000 miles
Ceiling: above 70,000 feet
Crew: one—pilot (two in trainer models)
Maximum takeoff weight: 40,000 pounds

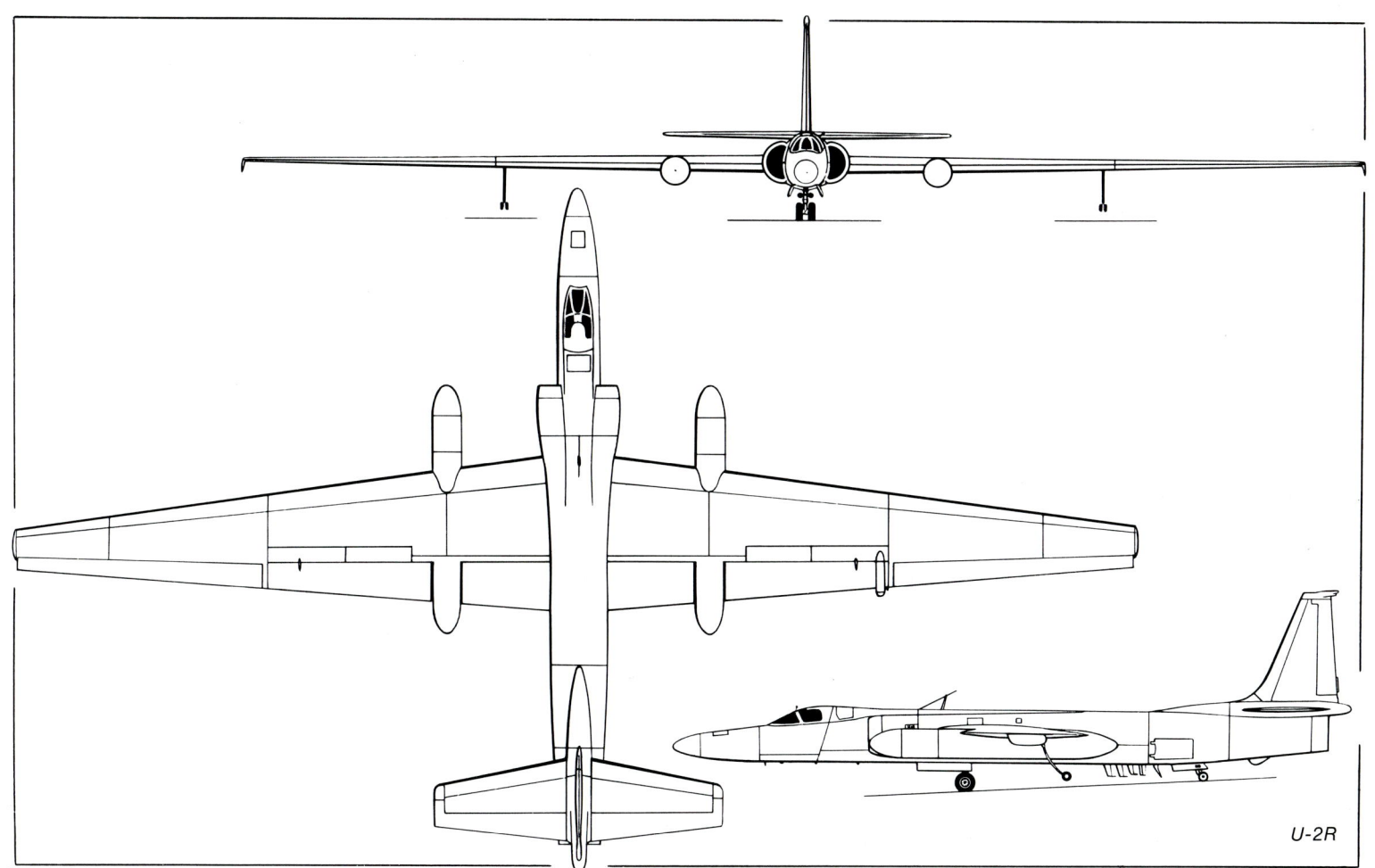

Photographs: p. 116, U-2R pilot; p. 117, U-2C (background); p. 118 inset, U-2R "wing walkers"; pp. 118-119, U-2R.

SR-71

USAF designation: SR-71
Nickname: Blackbird

The world's most advanced strategic reconnaissance aircraft, the SR-71 was delivered to the Strategic Air Command in January 1966. It is one of the fastest and highest-flying aircraft in the world today.

Operated by SAC's 9th Strategic Reconnaissance Wing at Beale Air Force Base near Marysville, California, the SR-71 is capable of both pre-attack and post-attack strategic reconnaissance. It carries a wide variety of advanced observation equipment and can survey over 100,000 square miles of the earth's surface in one hour from an altitude of 80,000 feet. With its advanced capabilities, the SR-71 out-performs all other reconnaissance aircraft.

In September 1974, an SR-71 flew from New York to London and from London to Los Angeles to establish two world speed records. The first was set on September 1, when Major James V. Sullivan, 37, a SAC pilot born in Wheeler, Montana, and Major Noel F. Widdifield, 33, a reconnaissance systems officer from Anderson, Indiana, flew the aircraft 3,490 miles—New York to London—in one hour, 56 minutes. The ground speed averaged 1,817 mph. Nearly three hours were cut off the former record set by a British F-4K fighter in 1969.

On Friday, September 13, Captain Harold B. Adams, 31, of Spokane, Washington, with Major William C. Machorek, 32, of Teaneck, New Jersey, reconnaissance systems officer, flew the SR-71 east-to-west across seven time zones from London to Los Angeles in a race with the sun. The three-hour, 47-minute flight established a record over the 5,645-mile route. An added aerial refueling over the longer distance produced a slower ground speed of 1,480 mph on the flight. The aircraft arrived—by California time—almost four hours before its London-time departure.

In July 1976, over the western United States, the SR-71 set new absolute and world class records: altitude in horizontal flight—85,069 feet, speed over a straight course—2,193.64 mph, and speed over a closed circuit—2,092.29 mph.

When preparing for a flight, crew members report to the 9th Strategic Reconnaissance Wing's unique Physiological Support Division (PSD) for a pre-flight physical, high protein meal, and briefings on weather and special mission characteristics. Once this procedure is completed, they are helped into their special flight gear by PSD technicians, who will stay with them until they are aboard the SR-71 and "plugged in" to its systems.

Supersonic missions are continually flown over parts of the United States to test the aircraft and its systems, and to maintain crew proficiency. Missions include air refuelings over corridors approved by the Federal Aviation Administration.

Primary function: strategic reconnaissance
Prime contractor: Lockheed Aircraft Corp.
Power plant/manufacturer: two Pratt and Whitney JT11D-20B (J58) turbojet engines with afterburners
Thrust: in excess of 30,000 pounds each engine
Dimensions: wingspan 55 feet 7 inches, length 107 feet 5 inches, height 18 feet 6 inches
Speed: more than 2,000 mph (Mach 3)
Ceiling: above 80,000 feet
Range: more than 2,000 miles; global with aerial refueling
Crew: two—pilot and reconnaissance systems officer
Maximum takeoff weight: CLASSIFIED

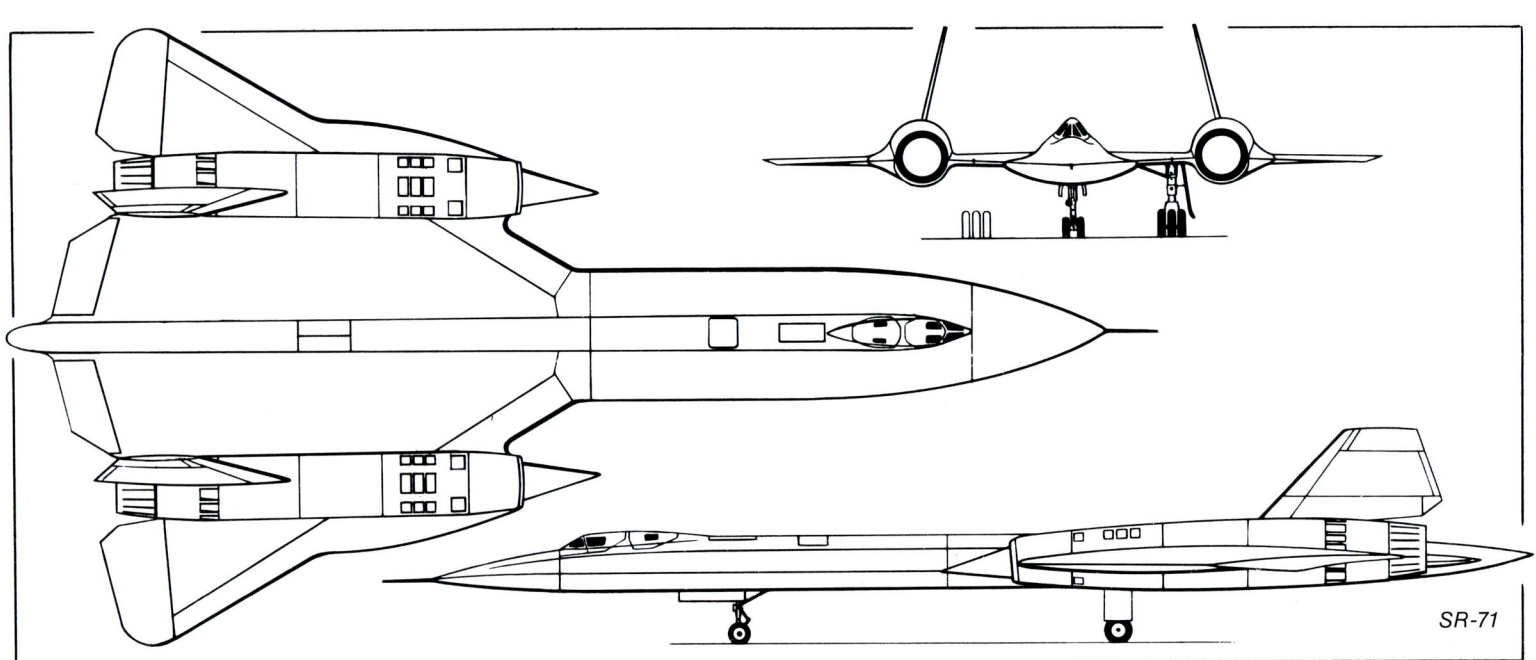

Photographs: pp. 8-9, SR-71B trainer; pp. 102-103, SR-71; pp. 104-105, SR-71; pp. 106-107, SR-71; p. 108, SR-71 pilot in cockpit; p. 109, SR-71; pp. 110-111, SR-71; p. 112, SR-71; p. 113, SR-71 pilot shoulder patch; pp. 114-115, SR-71; pp. 117, SR-71 (foreground).

E-3A

USAF designation: E-3A Sentry
Nickname: AWACS, Frisbee

The E-3A Sentry aircraft is an airborne warning and control system (AWACS) providing all-weather surveillance, command, control, and communications for commanders of United States and NATO tactical and air defense forces.

The E-3A is a modified Boeing 707 commercial airframe with a rotating radar dome supported eleven feet above the fuselage by two struts. The dome contains a radar system that permits surveillance from the earth's surface up into the stratosphere, over land or water. The radar has a range of more than 200 miles for low-flying targets and farther for aerospace vehicles flying at high altitudes. It can look down and detect, identify, and track enemy and friendly low-flying aircraft by eliminating ground clutter returns that confuse other radar systems.

The radar and computer systems on the E-3A can gather and present broad and detailed battlefield information. Systems operators sit at consoles displaying computer-processed data in graphic and tabular format. Information on the position and bearing of enemy aircraft and ships and the location and status of friendly aircraft, naval vessels, and ground troops is collected on board the E-3A. This data can be sent to major command and control centers in rear areas or aboard ships. In a crisis, vital elements of the data can be forwarded to National Command Authorities in the U.S.

For tactical purposes, the E-3A can provide information needed for interdiction, reconnaissance, airlift, and close-air support of friendly ground forces, as well as information enabling air-operations commanders to gain and maintain control of the skies.

As an air defense system, the Sentry can detect, identify, and track airborne enemy forces far from the boundaries of the U.S. and NATO countries. It can direct fighter interceptor aircraft to these enemy targets. The E-3A is a jam-resistant system that has performed missions under severe electronic countermeasures conditions. It is flexible and survivable. The Sentry can fly at high speeds for more than eleven hours without refueling. With its mobility, it has a greater chance of surviving in warfare than a fixed ground-based radar system. Its range and on-station time can be increased through in-flight refueling and the on-board rest area for the crew.

Engineering and test evaluation began on the first E-3A in October 1975. The 552nd Airborne Warning and Control Wing at Tinker Air Force Base, Oklahoma, received the first production E-3A in March 1977.

Primary function: airborne surveillance, command, control, and communications
Prime contractor: Boeing Aerospace Co.
Power plant/manufacturer: four Pratt and Whitney TF33-PW-100A turbofan engines
Thrust: 21,000 pounds each engine
Dimensions: wingspan 130 feet 10 inches, length 145 feet 6 inches, height 41 feet 4 inches, rotodome—30 feet diameter, 6 feet thick, mounted 11 feet above fuselage
Speed: more than 500 mph
Ceiling: above 29,000 feet
Endurance: more than 11 hours unrefueled
Crew: 17—four flight crew, 13 specialists according to mission
Maximum takeoff weight: 325,000 pounds

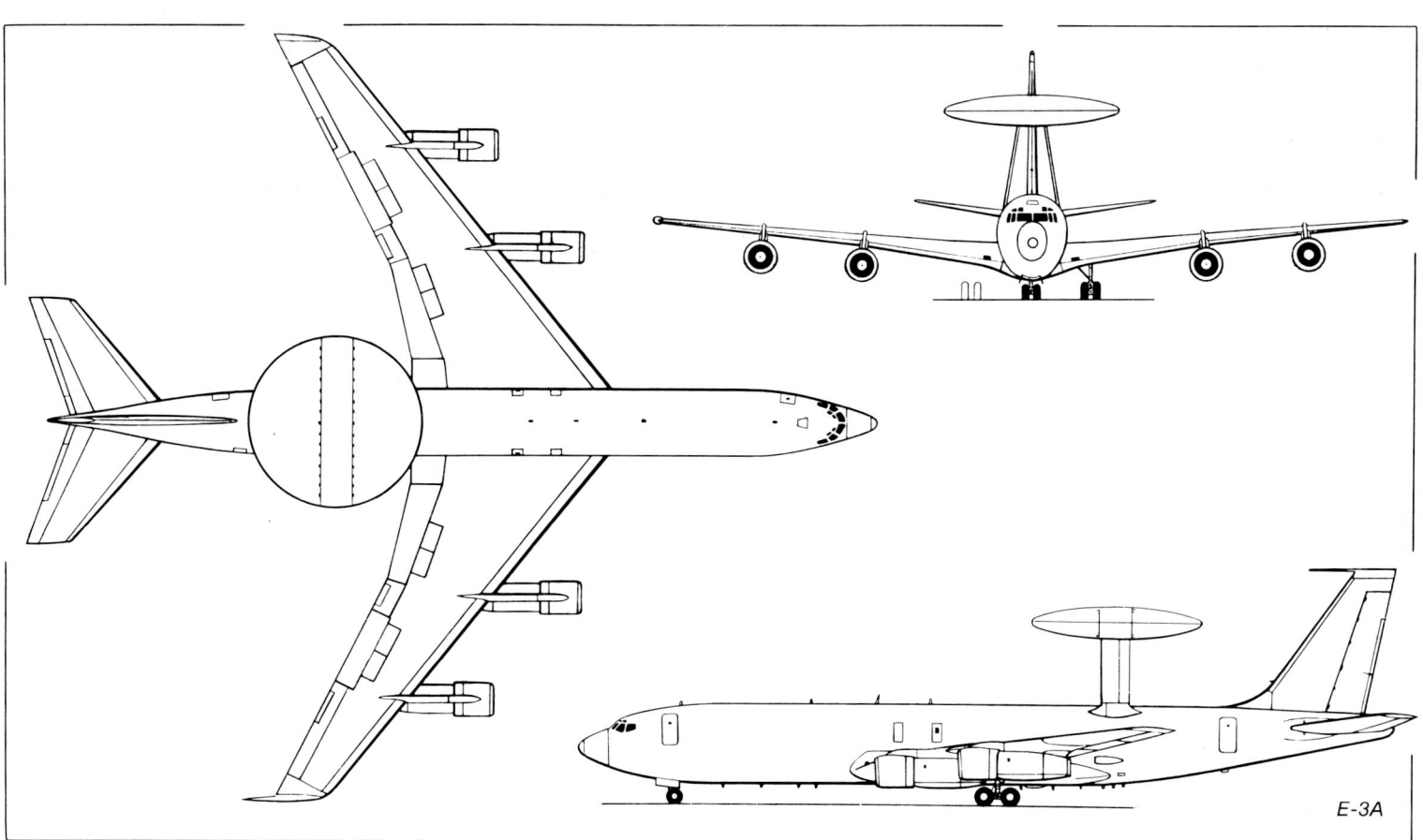

Photographs: p. 120, E-3A; p. 121, E-3A; pp. 122-123, E-3A being refueled by KC-135.

E-4

USAF designation: E-4A/B Airborne Command Post
Nickname: NEACP

In case of national emergency or the destruction of ground command centers, the E-4A/B Airborne Command Post assures a survivable means of executing the war orders of the United States National Command Authorities. The E-4A, a modified Boeing 747B jet transport, is currently utilized by the Joint Chiefs of Staff as the National Emergency Airborne Command Post (NEACP).

The mission of the NEACP is to support the President, Secretary of Defense, and the Joint Chiefs of Staff during a general war. The E-4A provides enhanced operational capabilities and increased survivability for the NEACP mission. While the Joint Chiefs of Staff control aircraft operations and man the command center aboard the E-4, the U.S. Air Force provides aircrew, logistics, and communications support primarily through the Strategic Air Command.

The E-4 plays the dual role of serving both the NEACP and the SAC Airborne Command Post missions. E-4Bs are similarly configured to the E-4A, making the aircraft readily interchangeable between the NEACP mission and the SAC Airborne Command Post mission. For SAC, the E-4 provides command control, battle staff operations, and communications capability.

Designed for long-endurance missions, the E-4A carries nearly three times the payload of its predecessor, the EC-135. The main deck of the aircraft is divided into six functional areas: the NCA work area, conference room, briefing room, battle staff work area, communications control center, and rest area. The flight deck houses the cockpit, navigation station, and flight-crew rest area. Lobes beneath the main deck house a technical control facility and a limited on-board maintenance storage capability. The aircraft can be refueled air-to-air.

The E-4B has improved communications via tactical satellite systems relaying high-speed data to forces and airborne command posts worldwide. With Airborne Launch Control System (ALCS) equipment on board, the E-4B provides increased assurance of a continued capability to effect airborne launch of the Minuteman missile force. Automatic data processing interfaced with space sensors and other electronic systems significantly increase the command and control capability of U.S. strategic forces.

SAC is the single support manager of the E-4 for the Air Force. The main operating location for all E-4s is Offutt Air Force Base, Nebraska.

Primary function: airborne command post
Prime contractor: The Boeing Company
Power plant/manufacturer: four General Electric CF6-50E engines
Thrust: 52,500 pounds each engine
Dimensions: wingspan 195 feet 8 inches, length 231 feet 4 inches, height 63 feet 5 inches, floor space—4,350 square feet
Speed: 679 mph
Ceiling: 45,100 feet
Endurance: unrefueled, in excess of 12 hours
Crew: up to 94, including flight crew
Maximum takeoff weight: 800,000 pounds

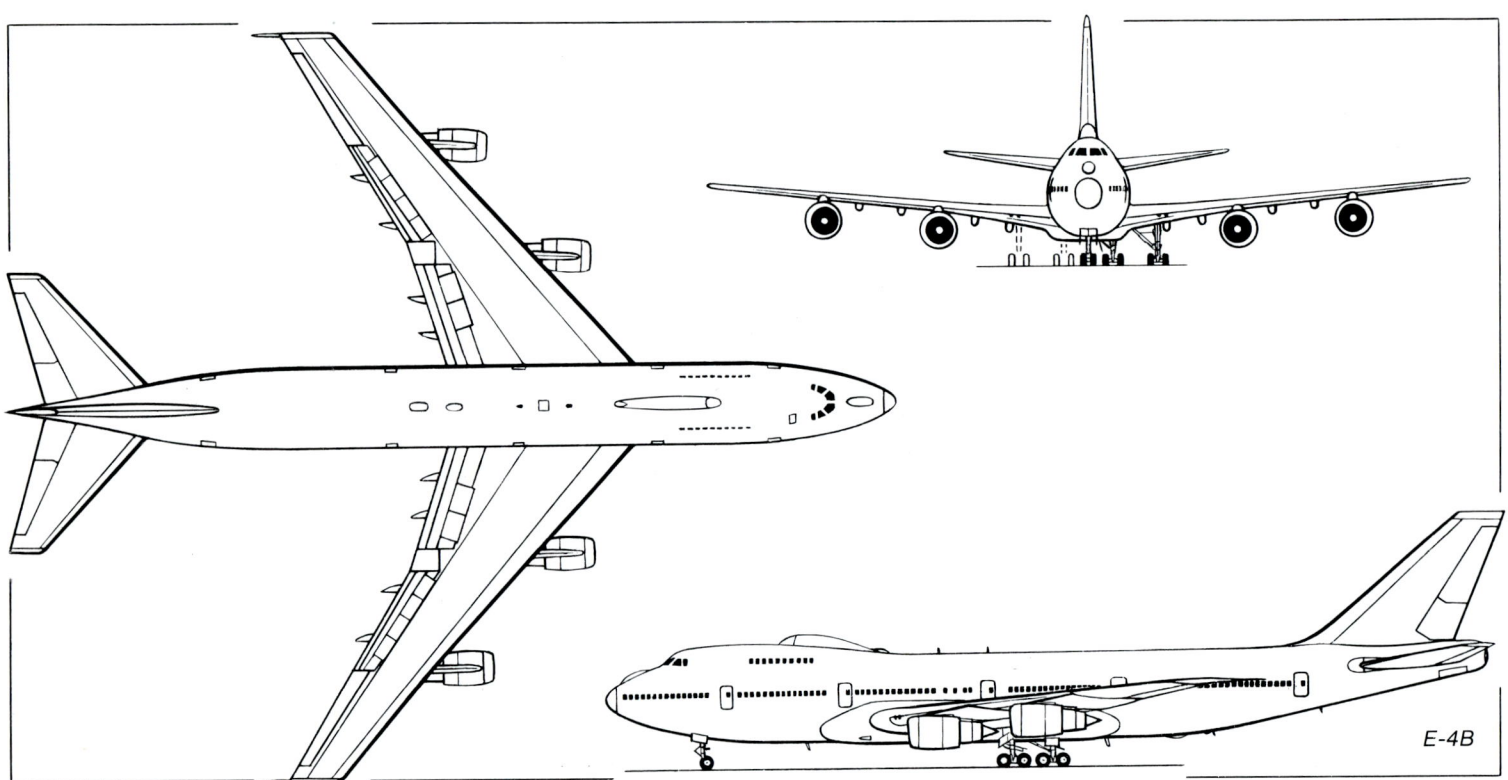

Photographs: p. 124, E-4B; pp. 124-125, E-4B; pp. 126-127, special NASA Boeing 747 modified to transport Space Shuttle—"Columbia" is aboard here.